Lecture Notes in Computer Science 6010

Commenced Publication in 1973
Founding and Former Series Editors:
Gerhard Goos, Juris Hartmanis, and Jan van Leeuwen

Yun Q. Shi (Ed.)

Transactions on Data Hiding and Multimedia Security V

Springer

Volume Editor

Yun Q. Shi
New Jersey Institute of Technology
University Heights, Newark, NJ, 07102-1982, USA
E-mail: shi@njit.edu

Library of Congress Control Number: Applied for

CR Subject Classification (1998): K.6.5, E.3, C.2, D.4.6, I.4, I.5

LNCS Sublibrary: SL 1 – Theoretical Computer Science and General Issues

ISSN 0302-9743 (Lecture Notes in Computer Science)
ISSN 1864-3043 (Transactions on Data Hiding and Multimedia Security)
ISBN-10 3-642-14297-4 Springer Berlin Heidelberg New York
ISBN-13 978-3-642-14297-0 Springer Berlin Heidelberg New York

springer.com

Printed in Germany

Typesetting: Camera-ready by author, data conversion by Scientific Publishing Services, Chennai, India
Printed on acid-free paper 06/3180

Preface

This issue contains a special section on "Forens ic Image Analysis for Crime Prevention," edited by Yan, Bouridane and Kankanhalli, containing two papers. In addition, the issue also contains four regular papers. The first paper by Cha and Kuo reviews recent development of multi-carrier code division multi-access (MC-CDMA)-based fingerprinting systems, presents new results on capacity, throughput, and distortion of a colluded media file, and points out important open research problems. To prevent illegal matching, Ito and Kiya propose in the second paper a phase correlation-based image matching in scrambled domain. The last two papers by Weir and Yan deal with visual cryptography. In the former, a comprehensive survey on visual cryptography is presented, which summarizes the latest developments, introduces the main research topics, and outlines directions and trends for future research. In the latter, a more powerful visual cryptographic scheme is proposed, in which multiple secrets are considered and a key share is generated for all the secrets.

We hope that this issue is of great interest to the research community and will trigger new research in the field of data hiding and multimedia security. Finally, we want to thank all the authors, reviewers, editors and special section organizers, who have devoted their valuable time to the success of this fifth issue. Special thanks go to Springer and Alfred Hofmann for their continuous support.

April 2010

Yun Q. Shi (Editor-in-Chief)
Hyoung-Joong Kim (Vice Editor-in-Chief)
Stefan Katzenbeisser (Vice Editor-in-Chief)

LNCS Transactions on Data Hiding and Multimedia Security

Editorial Board

Kivanc Mihcak	Bogazici University, Istanbul, Turkey kivanc.mihcak@boun.edu.tr
Hideki Noda	Kyushu Institute of Technology, Iizuka, Japan noda@mip.ces.kyutech.ac.jp
Jeng-Shyang Pan	National Kaohsiung University of Applied Sciences, Kaohsiung, Taiwan jspan@cc.kuas.edu.tw
Fernando Perez-Gonzalez	University of Vigo, Vigo, Spain fperez@gts.tsc.uvigo.es
Andreas Pfitzmann	Dresden University of Technology, Germany pfitza@inf.tu-dresden.de
Alessandro Piva	University of Florence, Florence, Italy piva@lci.det.unifi.it
Yong-Man Ro	Information and Communications University, Daejeon, Korea yro@icu.ac.kr
Ahmad-Reza Sadeghi	Ruhr-University, Bochum, Germany sadeghi@crypto.rub.de
Kouichi Sakurai	Kyushu University, Fukuoka, Japan sakurai@csce.kyushu-u.ac.jp
Edward Wong	Polytechnic University, Brooklyn, NY, USA wong@poly.edu

Advisory Board

Pil Joong Lee	Pohang University of Science and Technology, Pohang, Korea pjl@postech.ac.kr
Bede Liu	Princeton University, Princeton, NJ, USA liu@ee.princeton.edu

Introduction to the Special Section on Forensic Image Analysis for Crime Prevention

WeiQi Yan, Queen's University Belfast, UK
Ahmed Bouridane, Northumbria University, UK
Mohan S. Kankanhalli, National University of Singapore, Singapore

Digital image forensics involves performing complex analysis tasks on a large set of image data, which are of usually low quality, to detect useful and highly discriminative patterns. Pattern recognition has been suggested as a possible solution, and a lot of research has been devoted to the development of highly efficient systems for digital image forensic problems.

This special section on "Forensic Image Analysis for Crime Prevention" aims at presenting some of the recent research results in the area of digital image forensics. The objective of this special section is to highlight some quality research efforts that address the challenges in the emerging area of image-based evidence for forensic science and crime prevention applications with a view to provide the readers (researchers and forensic scientists) with an overview of the state of the art in this field. After several rounds of reviews, two papers were selected for publication in this special section.

The first contribution introduces partial palmprint matching using invariant local minutiae descriptors. In forensic investigations, it is common for forensic investigators to obtain a photograph of evidence left at the scene of crimes to aid them catch the culprit(s). Although fingerprints are the most popular evidence that can be used, crime scene officers claim that more than 30% of the evidence recovered from crime scenes originates from palms. Usually, the palmprint evidence left at crime scenes is partial with full palmprints obtained very rarely. In particular, partial palmprints do not exhibit a structured shape and often do not contain a reference point that can be used for their alignment to achieve efficient matching. This makes conventional matching methods based on alignment and minutiae pairing, as used in fingerprint recognition, to fail in partial palmprint recognition problems. In this paper, a new partial-to-full palmprint recognition approach based on invariant minutiae descriptors is proposed where the partial palmprint's minutiae are extracted and considered as the distinctive and discriminating features for each palmprint image. This is achieved by assigning to each minutiae a feature descriptor formed using the values of all the orientation histograms of the minutiae at hand. This allows for the descriptors to be rotation invariant, thus avoiding any image alignment at the matching stage. The results obtained show that the proposed technique yields a recognition rate of 99.2%. The solution can potentially provide high confidence to judicial juries in their deliberations and decisions.

The second contribution is concerned with color-based tracing in real-life surveillance data where variations in viewpoint, light source, background and shading are encountered. Tracing is a new problem in the area of surveillance video analytics – it is related to, but is substantially different from, tracking. Given that a suspect can be captured on multiple cameras distributed over time and space, tracing aims to link the tracked person across such multiple data collections. All these variations in ambient conditions impact on the appearance of the person in the data in many ways. Moreover, the suspect can deliberately alter his appearance in order to avoid detection. To develop automated systems for analytics, methods needed are that are robust to all these variations. In this paper, the authors discuss what types of invariance can be introduced to deal with these variations. They discuss tracing methods that can use these invariance characteristics to deal with real-life data and show that tracing algorithms can obtain better results if the algorithm is made invariant to specific changes in the data. This empirical work is a first toward developing robust tracing algorithms.

Both of the papers in this section were selected after stringent peer review and expert scrutiny. It represents the leading front of research in this very vital area of forensic image analysis. Overcoming the challenging research problems in this area requires a significant amount of intellectual resources, but we are very confident that it will attract substantial efforts in the future. In a certain sense, this special section is a small sampler of the exciting future of digital forensics.

Table of Contents

Forensic Image Analysis for Crime Prevention

Partial Palmprint Matching Using Invariant Local Minutiae Descriptors 1
Moussadek Laadjel, Ahmed Bouridane, Fatih Kurugollu, Omar Nibouche, and WeiQi Yan

Color Based Tracing in Real-Life Surveillance Data 18
Michael J. Metternich, Marcel Worring, and Arnold W.M. Smeulders

Regular Papers

Collusion-Resistant Fingerprinting Systems: Review and Recent Results 34
Byung-Ho Cha and C.-C. Jay Kuo

Phase-Only Correlation Based Matching in Scrambled Domain for Preventing Illegal Matching 51
Izumi Ito and Hitoshi Kiya

A Comprehensive Study of Visual Cryptography 70
Jonathan Weir and WeiQi Yan

Secure Masks for Visual Cryptography 106
Jonathan Weir and WeiQi Yan

Author Index 129

Partial Palmprint Matching Using Invariant Local Minutiae Descriptors

Moussadek Laadjel[1,*], Ahmed Bouridane[2,3], Fatih Kurugollu[1], Omar Nibouche[1], and WeiQi Yan[1]

[1] The Institute of Electronics, Communications and Information Technology
Queen's University Belfast
Belfast BT3 9DT, United Kingdom
mlaadjel01@qub.ac.uk

[2] School of Computing, Engineering and Information Sciences, Northumbria University, Pandon Building, Newcastle upon Tyne NE2 1XE, United Kingdom

[3] College of Computer and Information Sciences, King Saud University P.O.Box 51178 Riyadh 11543, Kingdom of Saudi Arabia

Abstract. In forensic investigations, it is common for forensic investigators to obtain a photograph of evidence left at the scene of crimes to aid them catch the culprit(s). Although, fingerprints are the most popular evidence that can be used, scene of crime officers claim that more than 30% of the evidence recovered from crime scenes originate from palms. Usually, palmprints evidence left at crime scenes are partial since very rarely full palmprints are obtained. In particular, partial palmprints do not exhibit a structured shape and often do not contain a reference point that can be used for their alignment to achieve efficient matching. This makes conventional matching methods based on alignment and minutiae pairing, as used in fingerprint recognition, to fail in partial palmprint recognition problems. In this paper a new partial-to-full palmprint recognition based on invariant minutiae descriptors is proposed where the partial palmprint's minutiae are extracted and considered as the distinctive and discriminating features for each palmprint image. This is achieved by assigning to each minutiae a feature descriptor formed using the values of all the orientation histograms of the minutiae at hand. This allows for the descriptors to be rotation invariant and as such do not require any image alignment at the matching stage. The results obtained show that the proposed technique yields a recognition rate of 99.2%. The solution does give a high confidence to the judicial jury in their deliberations and decision.

Keywords: Minutiae Descriptor, Orientation Histogram, Partial Palmprint.

1 Introduction

Fingerprint identification has been around for a long time. It has nearly a century of deployment in different sectors ranging from commercial applications such as access control to forensic applications such as suspect searching and law enforcement. Fingerprint matching is accepted as one of the crucial steps in Automatic

* Corresponding Author.

Y.Q. Shi (Ed.): Transactions on DHMS V, LNCS 6010, pp. 1–17, 2010.

Fingerprint Identification System. Intense works have been carried out in the full-to-full fingerprint matching stage and can be divided into two methods: minutiae and correlation based techniques. The effectiveness of the correlation based techniques are highly reliant on image gray level and are very sensitive to non-linear distortions. On the other hand, minutiae based techniques attempt to align two sets of minutiae points and determine the total number of the matched minutiae [1][2][3][4]. In addition, partial-to-full fingerprint matching has attracted the attention of many researchers in the last few years and the algorithms [5] [6] are examples of such methods. Similar to partial fingerprint recognition researchers stated that palmprint biometric is very efficient for people identification and can be complementary to the fingerprint in some doubtful investigation cases. For example, ridge patterns present in human palms are a unique feature, permanent and are among the most reliable human characteristics that can be used for people identification. The most common features that can be extracted from ridges are the ridge endings and bifurcations refereed to as minutiae. The use of partial palmprint can be exploited to identify suspects since police investigators stated that 30% of the evidences left in the crime scene originate from palms [7]. It is also simple to ink or photograph the palm traces before sending them to forensic laboratories where they can be scanned and used for matching against existing databases. In this paper, a partial-to-full palmprint technique for use in forensic investigations is presented. Our technique aims to assign an invariant feature descriptor to each minutiae extracted from the partial palmprint. The feature descriptor is then matched against registered full palmprints with the number of the matched minutiae being the matching score. The main contribution of this paper is to combine the Scale Invariant Feature Transform (SIFT) algorithm [8] and minutiae points and proposes a set of invariant feature descriptors referred to as Invariant Local Minutiae Descriptors (ILMDs). The structure of ILMD comes to overcome the drawback of the minutiae paring used in fingerprint matching [1]. The proposed ILMD is capable to efficiently match a partial-to-full palmprint image under translation, rotation and illumination changes and does not require any prior alignment.

The proposed technique operates as follows: in the test stage, the partial palmprint image at hand is enhanced to improve the clarity of the ridges and the valley structures of the image. Then, the minutiae points are extracted and their location and type (ending or bifurcation) are recorded. The coordinates of the minutiae points are used to locate them in the palmprint image as follows: for each minutiae a surrounding area is sampled and a feature vector is constructed using the values of all the orientation histograms sets entries within a local area of 16×16 pixels width. Finally, a matching algorithm based on the minutiae type is also proposed to match a partial palmprint to the full once stored in a reference database. The results obtained and their analysis using 3 different partial palmprint databases infer that the proposed technique yields attractive results with an Equal Error Rate (EER) smaller than 0.8%.

The remainder of the paper is organized as follows: a review of SIFT algorithm including the motivations are described in section 2. Section 3 details the partial palmprint image enhancement while the minutiae extraction including their orientation histograms are explained in section 4. The construction of an ILMD is then described in section 5 while section 6 details the proposed matching algorithm. Section 7 discusses and analyzes the results obtained. Finally, a conclusion is drawn in section 8.

2 Scale Invariant Feature Transform

SIFT is a widely used method for finding corresponding points of interest between images, for instance for object recognition, with invariance to scale, rotation and illumination variations [8][9][10][11]. A SIFT descriptor is a 3D histogram of gradient locations and orientations. Usually, the location is quantized into a 4×4 grid and the gradient angle is quantized to 8 orientations giving a descriptor of 128 points. The descriptor is assigned to each point that exhibits minimum or maximum pixel intensity in a given neighborhood area, say of 9×9 across a scale space [8]. However, scale space extrema detection produces a large number of feature points in which some may not be stable and may lead to an efficient matching. In addition, representing each point using a 128-dimensional vector requires quite a high memory storage and computationally expensive processing. For example, a palmprint image of size 1024×1024 with a 500 dpi resolution would produce around 40,000 points which is a massive number requiring an enormous computing power for descriptors construction and points matching as can be seen in Fig.1(b). This massive number of the keypoints makes matching algorithm not practical for palmprint identification. To overcome this problem two solutions can be used: either reduce the descriptor dimension or instead reduce the number of the detected key points. *Herbert et al.*[12] in their early work claimed that reducing the descriptor's dimension leads to a loss matching

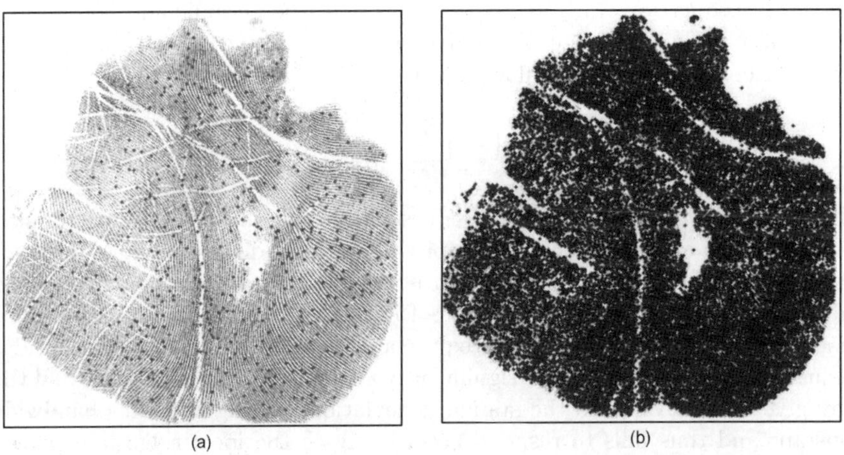

Fig. 1. (a) Minutiae feature points (Red points). (b) SIFT feature points (Blue points).

robustness . Therefore, in this paper we focus on the reduction of the feature key points before applying the SIFT to palmprint matching. Instead of finding the extrema in the palmprint images, we show that the minutiae points are visually significant, more robust and much smaller in number than SIFT key points, an average of 500 minutiae are obtained for the same palmprint image (Fig.1(a)). It is also worthwhile to mention that minutiae feature points are geometrically stable and their repeatability holds for any two different palmprint images of the same person taken under different conditions such as rotation, translation and illumination changes. Generally, poor quality palmprint images lead to the generation of spurious minutiae or the loss of some of them. To deal with this drawback, a prior palmprint image enhancement is necessary.

3 Image Enhancement and Minutiae Extraction

In order to ensure the robustness of the minutiae extraction with the inherent poor quality of partial palmprint images, an enhancement algorithm is necessary to improve the clarity of the ridges and the valley structures of the image. *Jain et al.*[13] have proposed a modified palmprint enhancement approach based on the algorithm proposed by Funada *et al.* [14] to remove the palmprint creases and to reliably extract the palm ridges. Their approach is based on Gabor filters and a region growing algorithm to connect the broken ridges in order to minimize the number of the false extracted minutiae. In this paper, a conventional algorithm used in fingerprint enhancement has been employed [15]. Which has given a satisfactory results for minutiae extraction relatively to the available images quality. The main steps of this algorithm are (i) image normalization (ii) local orientation estimation (iii) local frequency estimation (iv) region mask estimation (v) filtering using Gabor filters. This algorithm can be reliably used for palmprint enhancement since both palmprint and fingerprint exhibit a similar structure and is based on Gabor filter. Gabor filter has both frequency and orientation selectively properties which allows the capture of the periodic and non-periodic nature of a palmprint image. For a given frequency f and orientation θ, the 2D Gabor filter is given by the following equation:

$$G(x, y) = exp\{-\frac{1}{2}[\frac{x_0^2}{\sigma_x^2} + \frac{y_0^2}{\sigma_y^2}]\} \cdot \cos(2\pi f x_0) \tag{1}$$

where $x_0 = x\sin(\theta)+y\cos(\theta)$, $y_0 = -x\cos(\theta)+y\sin(\theta)$ and $(\sigma_x,\ \sigma_y)$ are the standard deviation of the Gaussian envelopes along the X-direction and Y-direction, respectively. The value of f and θ can be estimated from the palmprint image subregion. A problem with these type of filters however, is that, since they are tuned to specific frequencies, they require a preliminary estimation of the ridges frequency. Frequency may vary significantly across the palmprint image and thus may give a fixed value to the standard deviation making the filter bandwidth constant and thus fails to respond accordingly to the local ridge frequency of the palmprint image. To address this problem, the value of σ_x and σ_y have been chosen as a function of the ridge frequency $F(i, j)$ using the following forms

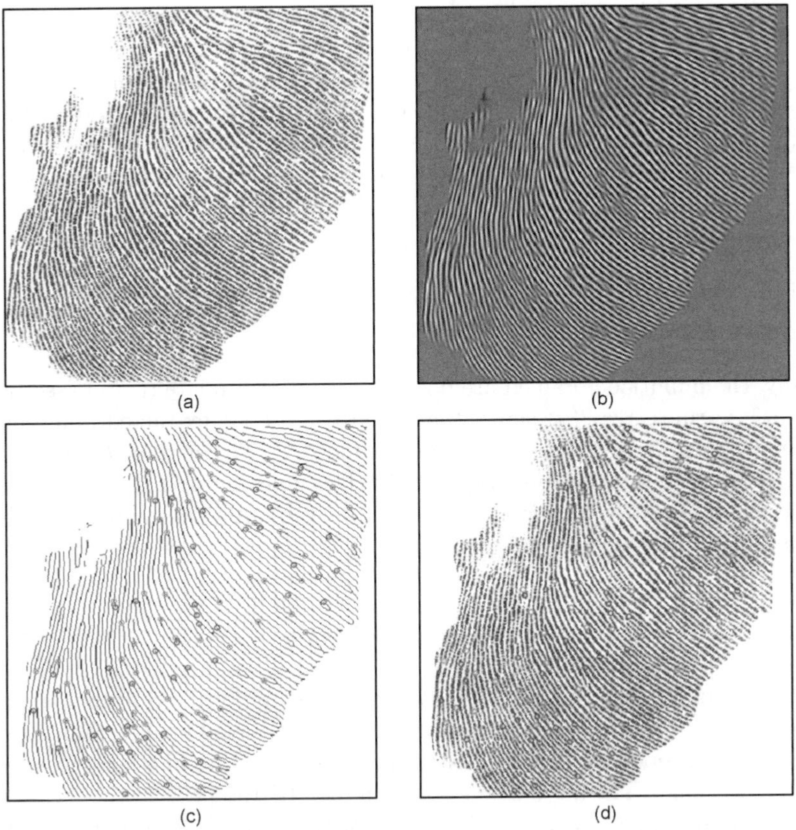

Fig. 2. Results of minutia extraction algorithm on a partial palmprint image taken by an inkless scanner. (a) Partial palmprint. (b) Image enhancement. (c) Image thinning. (d) Minutiae extraction.

$\sigma_x = K_x \cdot F(i,j)$ and $\sigma_x = K_x \cdot F(i,j)$ which allows us to reduce spurious ridges and valleys (see Fig.2(b)). (K_x, K_y) are constant variables chosen empirically equal to $(0.5, 0.5)$.

Once palmprint image enhancement is done, minutiae extraction follows. The two most prominent local ridge characteristics, called minutiae are (i) ridge endings (ii) ridge bifurcations. A ridge ending is defined as the point where a ridge ends abruptly while a ridge bifurcation is defined as the point in which a ridge diverges into branch ridges [15]. Minutiae extraction requires first the conversion of the enhanced palmprint image into a binary image using a global threshold T and assigning each pixel a value according to the following equation [16]:

$$I_b(x,y) = \begin{cases} 1 & \text{if } I(x,y) > T \\ 0 & \text{if } I(u,v) \leq T \end{cases} \tag{2}$$

where $I(x,y)$ is the enhanced palmprint image, usually a thinning algorithm is required after image binarization to obtain the skeleton of the palmprint image (see Fig.2(c)). Once a binary skeleton is obtained the minutiae extraction becomes a simple task. Let us assume that the foreground skeleton and the background are of values 1 and 0, respectively. Minutiae can be extracted by investigating the eight neighborhood of ridge skeleton using a Crossing Number (CN) algorithm which considers the 8 neighborhood of the ridge skeleton pixel at (i,j) and classifies it as follows: [17][18]:

- Ridge ending if $\sum_{i,j=-1}^{1} I(x+i, j+1) = 2$
- Ridge bifurcation if $\sum_{i,j=-1}^{1} I(x+i, j+1) = 4$

Finally, the minutiae obtained are post-processed to validate them based on set of heuristic rules. Fig.2(d) shows that almost all of the extracted minutiae are true minutiae. The extracted minutiae are indexed by $'En'$ and $'Bi'$ if they are ridge endings or bifurcations, respectively. The indexing operation will be used in the matching stage to decrease the number of minutiae mismatching and also to minimize the matching time.

4 Minutiae Orientation Assignment

Once the minutiae coordinates are obtained, they are localized in the palmprint image and an orientation or multi-orientation based local image gradient is applied. Let us suppose that the minutiae point is the center of a local window W within the image. The orientation is determined by the peak in the local orientation histogram. An orientation histogram with 36 bins is formed with each bin covering 10 degrees. Each sample point around the minutiae within W added to the histogram bin is weighted by its gradient magnitude and by a Gaussian-weighted circular window with a standard deviation σ of 3 (empirically chosen). The gradient magnitude and the orientation of the local points are computed using the following equations:

$$M(x,y) = \sqrt{(\frac{\partial I_B}{\partial x})^2 + (\frac{\partial I_B}{\partial y})^2} \quad (3)$$

$$\theta(x,y) = \tan^{-1}(\frac{\partial I_B}{\partial y} / \frac{\partial I_B}{\partial x}) \quad (4)$$

where I_B is the Gaussian blurred palmprint image given by equ.(5). The peaks in the orientation histogram correspond to the dominant orientations of the minutiae. Once the histogram is filled, the orientations corresponding to the highest peaks and local peaks that are within 80% of the highest peak are assigned to the minutiae. In the case of multiple orientations being assigned, an additional minutiae is created having the same location as the original one for each additional orientation. Assigning one or more orientations to the minutiae guarantee invariance to rotation as the minutiae descriptor is represented relative to

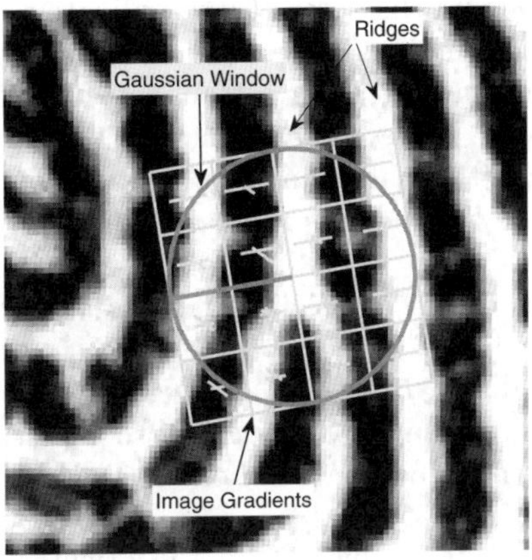

(a)

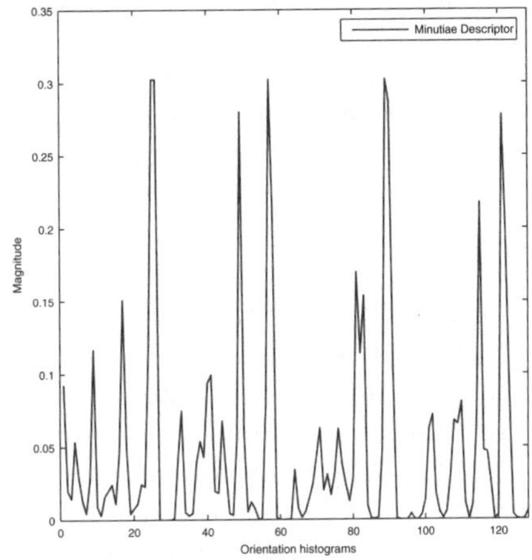

(b)

Fig. 3. Invariant Local Minutiae Descriptor. (a) Minutiae descriptor is created by first computing the gradient magnitude and orientation at each image sample point in a region around the minutiae location weighted by a Gaussian window indicated by the yellow circle. (b) These samples are then accumulated into a set of orientation histograms over 16 subregions of 4x4 pixels width around the minutiae.

this orientation. For example for multiple orientations assignment, the partial palmprint image shown in Fig.2 contains 119 minutiae extracted using the CN algorithm. However, 173 minutiae have been taken in consideration since some minutiae have assigned more than one orientation.

5 Invariant Local Minutiae Descriptor

In the previous section, orientations and locations were assigned to every minutiae. This ensures invariance to image translation and rotation since all the properties of the minutiae will be computed relative to the minutiae location and orientation. Now, similar to the work archived by Lowe [8], a descriptor vector is attributed to each minutiae. This descriptor has proven to be of high distinctness for many recognition tasks [19] [20]. The feature descriptor is computed as a set of the orientation histograms of 4×4 pixel neighborhoods relatively to the minutiae orientation. The descriptor is a local image measure vector and is refereed to as ILMD and is determined as follows [8]:

- **Step 1:** Blur the palmprint image using a Gaussian filter G with a standard deviation σ of $\sqrt{2}$ using equation (5).

$$I_{Blured} = G(x, y, \sigma) * I(x, y) \tag{5}$$

- **Step 2:** Sample the image gradient magnitude $M(x, y)$ and orientation $\theta(x, y)$ around the minutiae.

- **Step 3:** Rotate the gradient orientation and the descriptor coordinate relative to the minutiae orientation to make the descriptor rotation invariant.
- **Step 4:** Weight the magnitude of each sample using a Gaussian function with a standard deviation σ_w equals to 3. This weighing function is used to avoid sudden changes in the descriptor with small changes in the position of the window and to give less importance to gradients that are far from the minutiae location.
- **Step 5:** Create orientation histograms over 4×4 sample regions allowing for large local shift.
- **Step 6:** Use trilinear interpolation to distribute the value of each gradient sample into adjacent histogram bins to avoid abrupt changes of the descriptor as gradient samples shift smoothly from being within one histogram to another or from one orientation to another.
- **Step 7:** Construct the descriptor using the values of all the orientation histograms sets entries within 4×4 array with 8 orientations bin for each. This results in 128 elements for each ILMD assigned to each minutiae in a local region of 16×16.
- **Step 8:** Reduce the illumination changes by normalizing the ILMD to a unit length.

A palmprint image is then represented by a set of ILMDs corresponding to each minutiae. Therefore, for n minutiae for a given palmprint image, an $n \times 128$ ILMDs are extracted and used to match it against the full palmprint database.

6 Invariant Local Minutiae Descriptors Matching

Matching a partial-to-full palmprint is the process of returning a similarity score between a partial and full palmprint image. The proposed matching algorithm considers the score as the number of the matched minutiae between the evidence and the reference palmprint image. Let us suppose $I_E(d1_E,\ d2_E,\ d3_E, ...\ dn_E)$ and $I_R(d1_R,\ d2_R,\ d3_R, ...\ dn_R)$ are the ILMDs of the evidence and the full palmprint images, respectively. To determine the number of the matched minutiae, each ILMD from the evidence palmprint image indexed as a minutiae ending $'En'$ is compared only with all the ILMDs of the reference image that are $'E'$ and vice versa for the minutiae type $'Bi'$ using an Euclidean distance. To further reduce the effect of the mismatched minutiae, the two nearest neighbors ILMDs found in the full reference image are compared. If the second nearest ILMD differs significantly from the first nearest neighbor ILMD, it is assumed that the ILMD is isolated in I_R space and therefore considered as a good match, otherwise the ILMD has no match in the reference palmprint image. According to our experiments, it is found that at least more than 7 minutiae have to be matched in order to consider the evidence and the full palmprint come from the same person. Fig.4, Fig.5 and Fig.6 show clearly this observation in three different matching scenarios where a poor genuine, good genuine and good imposter palmprint evidence are matched against a full reference palmprint images, respectively. The

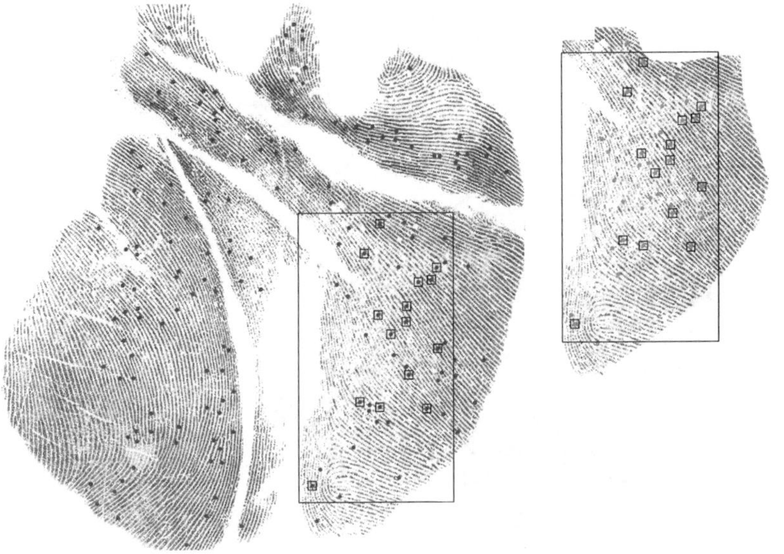

Fig. 4. Result of applying the matching algorithm to a genuine generated poor quality palmprint evidence

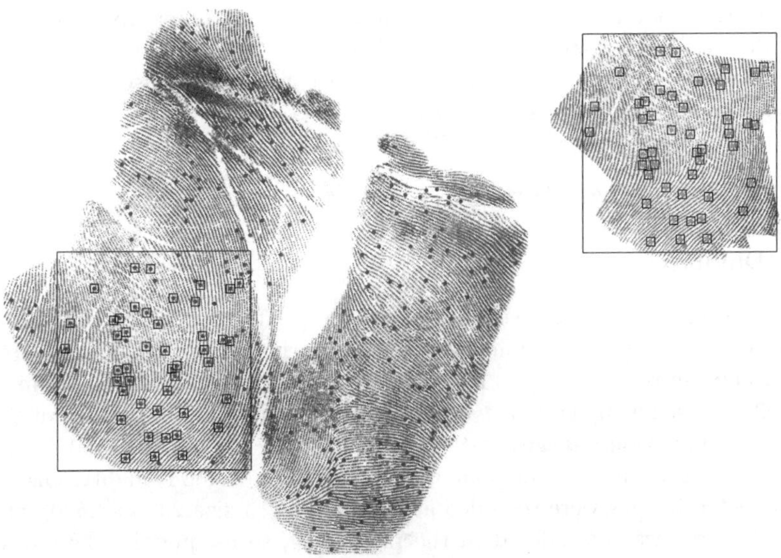

Fig. 5. Result of applying the matching algorithm to a genuine generated good quality palmprint evidence

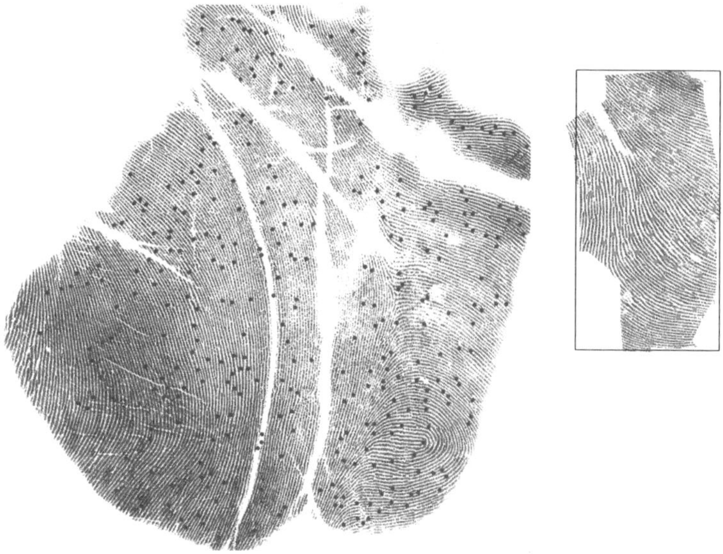

Fig. 6. Result of applying the matching algorithm to an imposter generated good quality palmprint evidence

small squares mean that the minutiae points are repeated and matched to each other in the evidence and reference palmprint images. It may be that a few of them do not have a match but their number is very small and does not affect the matching score. Therefore, the ILMD provides an efficient discrimination even for poor quality palmprints evidence.

7 Experimental Results

7.1 Database

All the experiments have been carried out on a database collected in our laboratory using a live scan scanner. 200 full palmprint images have been captured from 100 persons. Each person has been asked to provide two images of his right and left hands. The images have been captured without any environment control such as illumination changes and position. They are of varying quality impressions, ranging from those of poor quality to those of good quality. Originally, the collected images were recorded at 500 dpi and of size 2500×2500 but only the palm area was considered in the processing. Consequently, the size of all the images used in the following experiments was reduced to 1024×1024. The partial palmprints evidence were generated from the full palmprint images as follows: (i) 4 Quarters Palmprint (4QP) with an area of less than 25% of the full palmprint area (ii) 4 Half Palmprint (4HP) with an area of less than 50% of the full palmprint area (iii) 4 Random Palmprint (4RP) created using 4 different

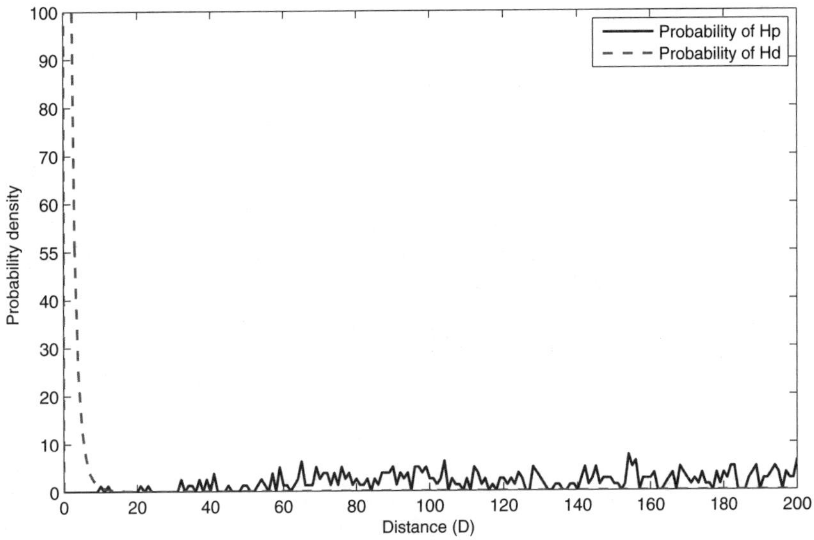

(a)

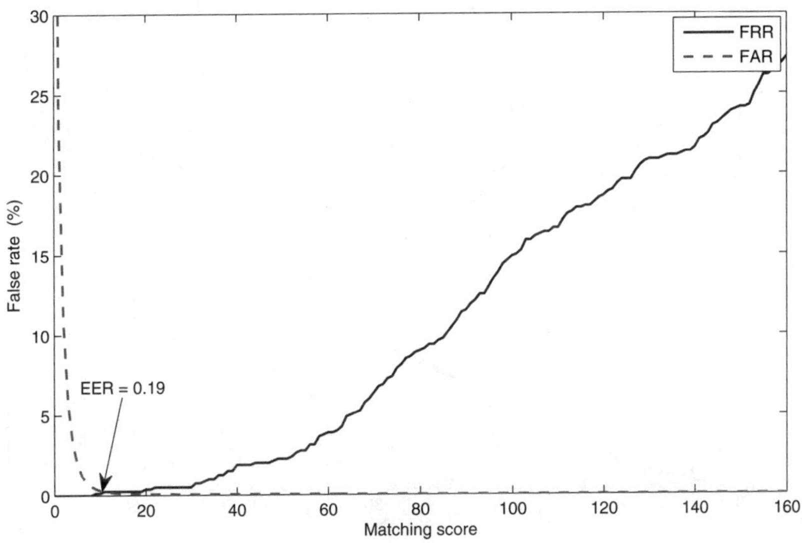

(b)

Fig. 7. (a) Probability distributions of H_p and H_d hypothesis using the 4HP testing database. (b) Corresponding ROC curve.

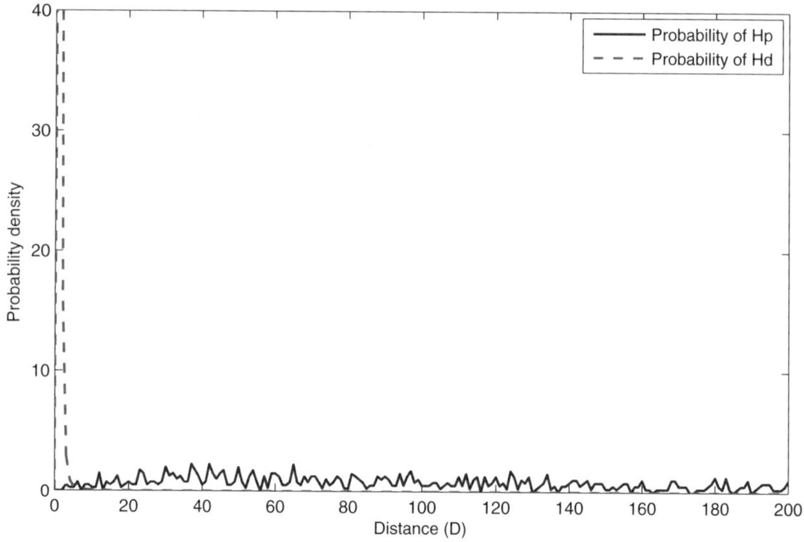

(a)

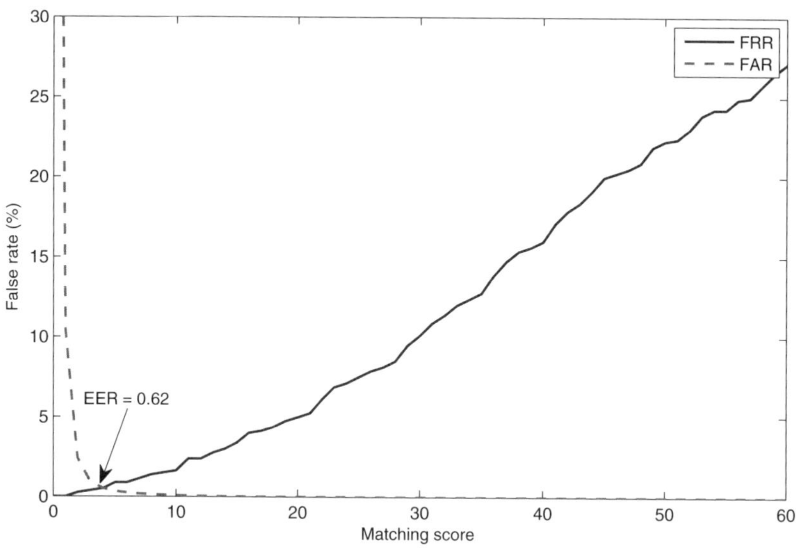

(b)

Fig. 8. (a) Probability distributions of H_p and H_d hypothesis using the 4QP testing database. (b) Corresponding ROC curve.

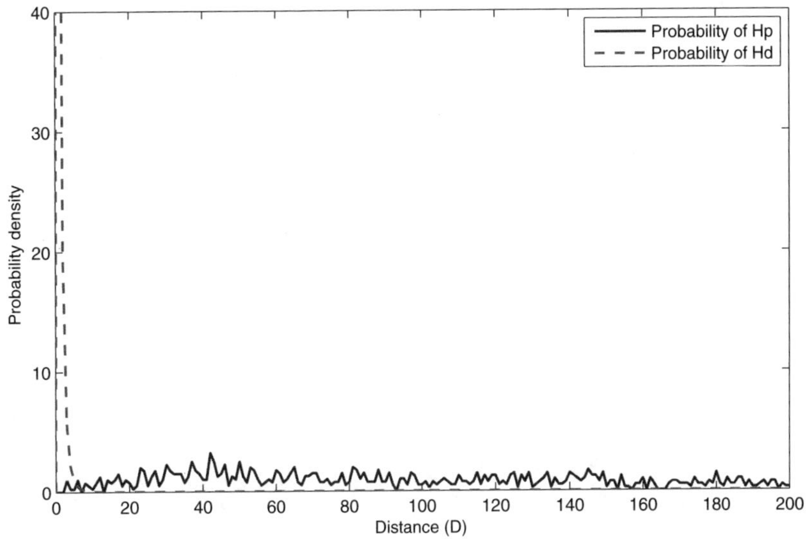

(a)

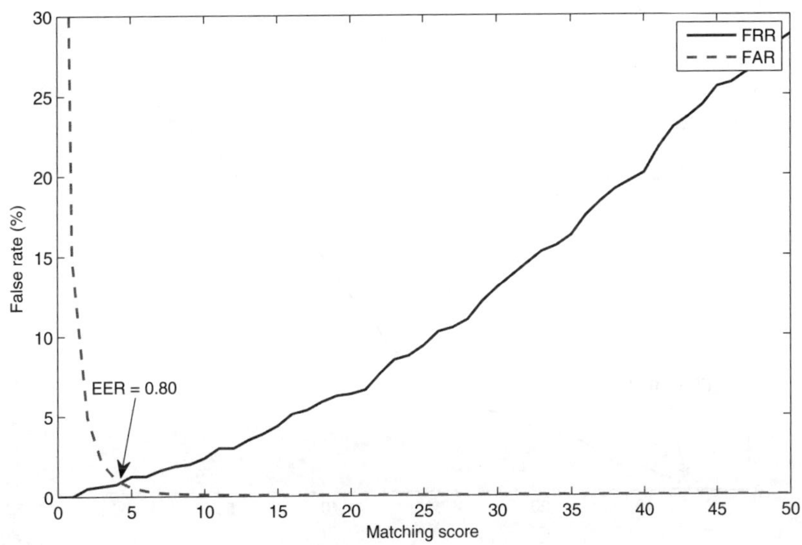

(b)

Fig. 9. (a) Probability distributions of H_p and H_d hypothesis using the 4RP testing database. (b) Corresponding ROC curve.

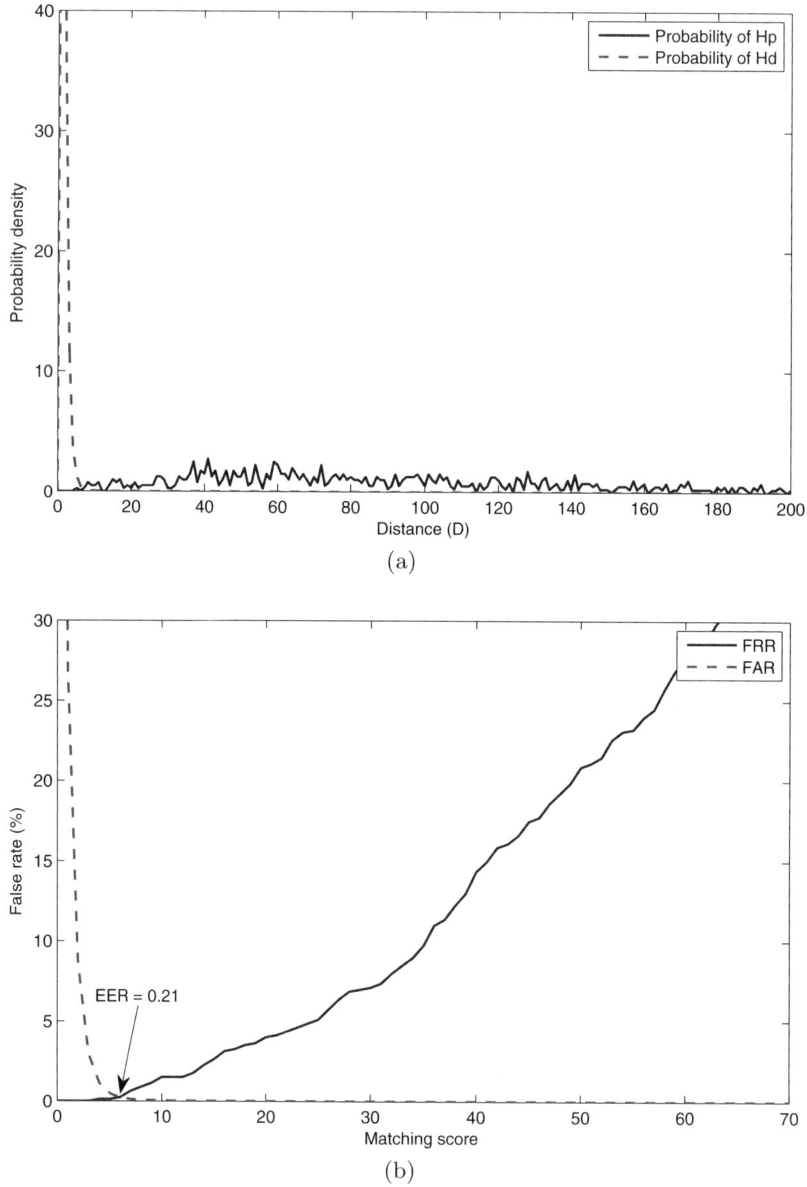

Fig. 10. (a) Probability distributions of H_p and H_d hypothesis of the SIFT algorithm using the 4RP testing database. (b) Corresponding ROC curve.

masks. In addition, these random palmprints were rotated by different angles of $15°, 30°, 45°, 60°$ and $90°$ and shifted vertically and horizontally.

7.2 Evaluation of the Strength of Evidence

To evaluate the strength of the partial palmprints evidence left at crime scenes, the probability that the palmprint evidence belong to either of the following hypothesis (i) H_p, the recovered evidence came from the suspect and (ii) H_d, the recovered evidence not came from the suspect have been used. In order to obtain H_p and H_d probability distributions, each test evidence was matched against all the full palmprint images in the reference database. Three different experiments have been carried on each test database 4HP, 4QP and 4RP. A matching is considered to fulfil the hypothesis H_p if the evidence palmprint and full palmprint are found to originate from the same person, otherwise it is considered to fulfil the hypothesis H_d. A total of 160,000 (200×800) matchings have been performed on each test database. The number of comparisons fulfils the hypothesis H_p is 800 and the remaining fulfils the hypothesis H_d. The probability distributions of H_p and H_d hypothesis are illustrated in Fig.7(a), Fig.8(a) and Fig.9(a) using the testing database 4HP, 4QP and 4RP, respectively. As can bee seen in these figures, H_p and H_d distributions are well sperate which means that the proposed technique easily distinguishes between evidences coming from the suspect targets and suspect non-targets. In this way, for any X-axis value each curve shows the number of matching minutiae. The greater the number of matching minutiae, the higher the strength of the evidence and the better the forensic system. To clearly shows the performance of the proposed technique, the False Acceptance Rate (FAR) which is the probability of accepting a wrong evidence as a correct one, the False Rejection Rate (FRR) which is the probability of rejecting a correct evidence as a wrong one and the EER which is the point where the FAR and FRR are equals have been used to measure the system performances. Fig.8(b), Fig.7(b) and Fig.9(b) depict the Receiver Operating Characteristics (ROC) curves which is the plot of the matching score against the FAR and FRR. As it shows, an EER of 0.19%,0.62% and 0.8% are obtained using the testing databases 4HP, 4QP and 4RP, respectively. The difference between the EERs is marginal thereby demonstrating the robustness and the invariance of the proposed ILMD and the matching procedure even in the case when the evidence palmprint is corrupted with geometrical distortions such as rotation and translation. Furthermore, it can also be seen that the area of the evidence or the number of the extracted minutiae slightly affect the matching robustness which is evidenced by the increase of the EER from 0.19% in the case of the 4HP database to 0.80% in the case of 4RP. For the purpose of comparison, the proposed approach is also compared with the SIFT technique proposed by Lowe [9]. Since Lowe's algorithm can not be implemented directly on our palmprint database due to the very large number of the detected keypoints as mentioned before, a solution will be to downsample the palmprint images and decrease their size from 1024×1024 to 512×512 before applying SIFT algorithm. By downsampling the palmprint images the number of the detected keypoints from around 40.000 to around 2.000 which is relatively

Table 1. Complexity comparison between SIFT and our proposed technique

	SIFT without downsampling	SIFT with downsampling	Proposed technique
Average number of detected points	40000	2000	500
Assigned descriptor length	128	128	128
Number of matching operations	40000×40000	2000×2000	less than 500×500

acceptable in terms of processing time for partial-to-full palmprint identification applications. Fig.10 shows the ROC curve of the SIFT algorithm using the 4RP testing database. As it can be seen, an EER of 0.21% is obtained which is not far from the EER obtained using the proposed technique. The small difference between both techniques is due to the inherently larger number of the keypoints detected using SIFT algorithm. However, our proposed technique is much less computationally intensive since the descriptors assignment and matching times are related to the number of the detected interesting points (minutiae and SIFT keypoints) in the palmprint image as explained in table.1. This table gives a clear comparison between our proposed technique and SIFT algorithm in terms of number of operations performed to match two palmprint images. For instance, in the matching stage it is clear that our technique is at least 16 times faster than the SIFT algorithm implemented on a downsampled palmprint images.

8 Conclusion

In this paper a new partial-to-full palmprint recognition technique for use in forensic problems is proposed. This is particularly of interest since matching partial palmprints evidence has not yet been widely exploited. This technique uses a well known modified algorithm (i.e., SIFT) to describe the extracted minutiae points and generate invariant local minutiae descriptors. The main advantage of the proposed technique is its robustness against rotation, translation and illumination changes. Furthermore, the proposed matching algorithm is faster compared to that of SIFT since only the same minutiae type are matched against each other (ending with ending and bifurcation with bifurcation). The proposed technique shows attractive results in the case of partial-to-full palmprint and would be tested as well in the case of partial-to-full fingerprint in the future work.

References

1. Anil, J., Hong, L., Bolle, R.: On-line fingerprint verification. IEEE Transactions on Pattern Analysis and Machine Intelligence 19, 302–314 (1997)
2. Tong, X., Huang, J., Tang, X., Shi, D.: Fingerprint minutiae matching using the adjacent feature vector. Pattern Recognition Lettre 26, 1337–1345 (2005)

3. Tico, M., Kuosmanen, P.: Fingerprint matching using an orientation-based minutia descriptor. IEEE Transactions on Pattern Analysis and Machine Intelligence 25, 1009–1014 (2003)
4. Isenor, D.K., Zaky, S.G.: Fingerprint identification using graph matching. Pattern Recognition Lettre 19, 113–122 (1986)
5. Jea, T.Y.: Minutiae-based partial fingerprint recognition. PhD thesis, Buffalo, NY, USA, Adviser-Venugopal Govindaraju (2005)
6. Girgis, M.R., Sewisy, A.A., Mansour, R.F.: A robust method for partial deformed fingerprints verification using genetic algorithm. Expert Systems with Applications 36, 2008–2016 (2009)
7. Dewan, S.: Elementary, watson: Scan a palm, find a clue (2003), `http://www.nytimes.com/`
8. Lowe, D.G.: Distinctive image features from scale-invariant keypoints. International Journal of Computer Vision 60, 91–110 (2004)
9. Lowe, D.G.: Object recognition from local scale-invariant features. In: Proceedings of the International Conference on Computer Vision, vol. 2, p. 1150 (1999)
10. Mikolajczyk, K., Schmid, C.: Scale & affine invariant interest point detectors. International Journal of Computer Vision 60, 63–86 (2004)
11. Mortensen, E.N., Deng, H., Shapiro, L.: A sift descriptor with global context. In: Proceedings of the 2005 IEEE Conference on Computer Vision and Pattern Recognition, vol. 1 (2005)
12. Bay, H., Ess, A., Tuytelaars, T., Gool, L.V.: Speeded-up robust features (surf). Computer Vision and Image Understing 110, 346–359 (2008)
13. Jain, A., Feng, J.: Latent palmprint matching. To Appear on IEEE Transactions on Pattern Analysis and Machine Intelligence (2009)
14. Ichi Funada, J., Ohta, N., Mizoguchi, M., Temma, T., Nakanishi, K., Murai, A., Sugiuchi, T., Wakabayashi, T., Yamada, Y.: Feature extraction method for palmprint considering elimination of creases. In: Proceedings of the 14th International Conference on Pattern Recognition, p. 1849 (1998)
15. Hong, L., Wan, Y., Jain, A.: Fingerprint image enhancement: Algorithm and performance evaluation. IEEE Transactions on Pattern Analysis and Machine Intelligence 20, 777–789 (1998)
16. Amengual, J.C., Juan, A., Prez, J.C., Sez, S., Vilar, J.M.: Real-time minutiae extraction in fingerprint images. In: Proceedings of the 6th IEE International Conference on Image Processing and its Applications (1997)
17. Farina, A., Kovács-Vajna, Z.M., Leone, A.: Fingerprint minutiae extraction from skeletonized binary images. Pattern Recognition Lettre 32 (1999)
18. Zhao, F., Tang, X.: Preprocessing and postprocessing for skeleton-based fingerprint minutiae extraction. Pattern Recognition Lettre 40 (2007)
19. Bicego, M., Lagorio, A., Grosso, E., Tistarelli, M.: On the use of sift features for face authentication. In: Proceedings of the 2006 Conference on Computer Vision and Pattern Recognition Workshop, p. 35 (2006)
20. Wang, K., Ren, Z., Xiong, X.: Combination of wavelet and sift features for image classification using trained gaussion mixture model. In: Proceedings of the 2008 International Conference on Intelligent Information Hiding and Multimedia Signal Processing, pp. 79–82 (2008)

Color Based Tracing in Real-Life Surveillance Data

Michael J. Metternich, Marcel Worring, and Arnold W.M. Smeulders

ISLA-University of Amsterdam,
Science Park 107, 1098 XG Amsterdam, The Netherlands
{M.J.Metternich,M.Worring,A.Smeulders}@uva.nl
http://www.science.uva.nl/research/isla/

Abstract. For post incident investigation a complete reconstruction of an event is needed based on surveillance footage of the crime scene and surrounding areas. Reconstruction of the whereabouts of the people in the incident requires the ability to follow persons within a camera's field-of-view (tracking) and between different cameras (tracing). In constrained situations a combination of shape and color information is shown to be best at discriminating between persons. In this paper we focus on person tracing between uncalibrated cameras with non-overlapping field-of-view. In these situations standard image matching techniques perform badly due to large, uncontrolled variations in viewpoint, light source, background and shading. We show that in these unconstrained real-life situations, tracing results are very dependent on the appearance of the subject.

Keywords: Real-life Surveillance and Tracing.

1 Introduction

The two major applications of camera surveillance are real-time crime prevention and crime investigation after an incident has occurred. For the first type of application event detection [22,23] or aggression detection [6,30] are used to understand people's actions. For post incident investigation a complete reconstruction of the event is needed which additionally requires to follow persons within a camera's field-of-view (tracking) and between different cameras (tracing). A system aiding a human user in this process should therefore be able to perform both tracking and tracing.

Person tracking is a very lively research area, with various workshops and challenges organized each year such as Performance Evaluation of Tracking and Surveillance (PETS) and People Detection and Tracking workshop of the 2009 IEEE International Conference on Robotics and Automation. Though this subject is far from solved, impressive results have been obtained in constrained as well as real-life situations. Note, however, that surveillance data is often time-lapsed and in these conditions tracking algorithms cannot be used as is, but need reconsideration or adaptation[15]. For an excellent overview of available tracking methods and their advantages and disadvantages, see [29].

Y.Q. Shi (Ed.): Transactions on DHMS V, LNCS 6010, pp. 18–33, 2010.

Up to now, studies regarding tracing have only been tested in controlled conditions. The major issues of real-life surveillance situations however, are the large, uncontrolled variation in viewpoint, light source and shading. These variations have great impact on the appearance of a person. Viewpoint changes affect the shape of the person as well as the colors of clothing as the observed color changes with the angle between light source and line of view. Changes in light source have direct impact on the color of any object and while shading does not change the color itself, it does change other characteristics like intensity or saturation. In constrained situations these challenges could be reduced by using pre-calibrated cameras [31,2] or by calibrating the cameras afterward using information about the overlapping field-of-view [4]. If the cameras are not calibrated and either the cameras' field-of-view do not overlap or it is unknown what the overlap is, any description usable for tracing should be able to deal with the lack of calibration. Color changes between cameras can be addressed by using color constancy methods [27] and various color spaces can be used to be invariant to shadows. These methods have been designed based on solid theoretical foundations and proven to be optimal in lab conditions. A major question is whether these methods generalize well enough to deal with the challenges of surveillance data, or that other criteria play a role there.

The paper is organized as follows. First, a state-of-the-art person detection system is described, which results are used throughout the paper. Section 3 introduces the tracing methods and invariance properties to answer the questions: How are image regions best described to be able to distinguish between persons? And (how) can unwanted variation in image regions be suppressed? The results of applying these methods to a benchmark and a real-life dataset are discussed in Section 4.

2 System Description

Any post incident investigation system is composed of at least three major steps. The first step is detection of persons in each of the cameras. The second step is to track these persons within a single camera. Afterward, these tracks are used to find instances of these persons in other cameras.

The standard approach for person detection is to match certain candidate detections to a model which is previously trained on sample images. One method to select these candidate detections is by simply selecting all regions over all frames of all possible sizes and locations. This is known as the sliding window technique. This method has two serious problems though: object classification is a time-consuming method, so classifying every possible sub-region of all frames in a dataset is infeasible. Another issue is that relying solely on classification scores will result in a great dependency on the chosen threshold. Both issues can be addressed by applying object classification only to certain regions of interest. The standard approach to obtain these regions of interest is background extraction; we use [32] for its ability to automatically optimize the number of components in a Gaussian Mixture Model. All regions of interest are described using Histograms of Oriented Gradients [5] and classified using a Support Vector Machine (SVM) classifier [28], previously trained on the INRIA dataset[1]. Regions of which the score exceeds some predefined threshold are then classified as persons. A known issue of only applying classification on non-static regions is that persons standing still cannot be detected. However, we focus on tracing persons; the only requirement on detections is therefore that each person was detected at least once.

To be able to combine the resulting detections into tracks either hysteresis thresholding can be used [15] or the detections can be used as initializations for a filtering method such as Kalman filtering [14]. While these methods will help in reducing the number of false positives and might lead to better representations, we do not use either method but focus on matching of singular image regions instead. The reason is that any method to combine the image regions will make errors, leading to paths containing two different persons or false positives as well as true positives. This might distract us from the goal of this paper, understanding how image regions should be matched.

If the camera's field of view is actively changed, results of various methods assuming static cameras are poor, e.g. background extraction. Before doing background extraction, we therefore automatically detect camera movement. The simple method we applied to detect these moments of camera movement is to measure the movement of salient points using sift features [19]. If the average movement is greater than some predefined threshold the camera is assumed to be moving. For the current paper these regions are excluded from further analysis. In practice, however, these parts could contain relevant information like zooming in on specific persons. Figure 1 shows an overview of this person detection system. A preliminary version of the system was published in [21].

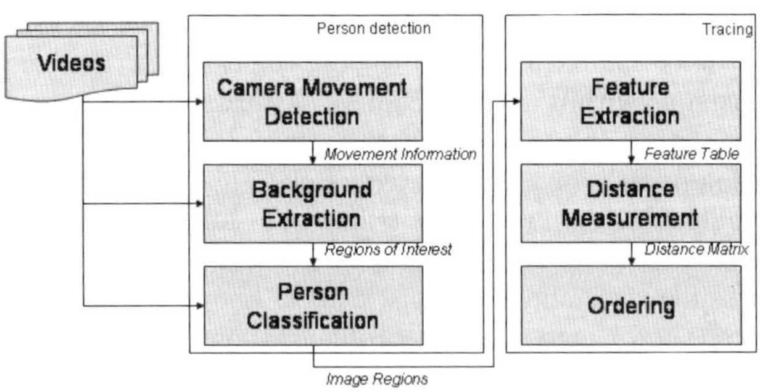

Fig. 1. Operational scheme of our person detection system

[1] This publicly available dataset can be downloaded from *http://pascal.inrialpes.fr/data/human/*

3 Tracing

We now use the image regions obtained from the person detection system described earlier to find image regions depicting the same person in other cameras. This can be studied using three techniques: image matching, image classification and image pair analysis. For image matching the image regions are described using predefined features, after which a comparison metric is used to order all image regions. Image classification uses similar features to represent an image region, but a classifier is specifically trained to distinguish between objects. The last method, image pair analysis, learns the most descriptive parts of an image regions autonomously, using manually defined image-region pairs [20]. These image regions are then used to identify a new object. The last two methods need specific training data of a person of interest. Instead of identifying persons, we aim to provide an overview of a dataset by helping the user to find multiple occurrences of a selected person. In these cases a classifier cannot be learned beforehand, so we focus on image matching techniques.

3.1 Feature Description

The simplest description of an image region is a global color histogram. This method ignores all location information and while this is very useful in many situations, it cannot make the vital distinction between a person wearing a red jacket and blue jeans and a person wearing a blue jacket and red jeans.

To obtain some location information Gray et al [12] introduced a 1D color histogram detected on predefined partitions of the image region. This method first divides the image in three parts: the top one fifth and middle and bottom two-fifths. For each sub-region three 1D histograms are calculated; the concatenated nine histograms are used as a descriptor for the complete image region.

In [1] an improvement of this descriptor is proposed which uses a collection of grids of region descriptors. Each grid segments the object into a different number of equally sized sub-rectangles. By combining fine regions with coarse regions, both local and global information is preserved.

Both methods are able to combine color and location information, but are unable to describe structure information such as patterns on a shirt. One method to capture shape, location and color information is the covariance matrix [25]. This method extracts a feature vector f_n for each pixel which are combined into the covariance matrix C of a region by:

$$C = \frac{1}{N-1} \sum_{n=1}^{N} (f_n - m)(f_n - m)^T \tag{1}$$

where N is the number of points in the region, m the mean vector of all the feature vectors and f_n the feature vector used to describe a position in the region. To measure the influence of different descriptor types, we use three types of feature vectors:

$$f_{shape} = C(x, y, I, I_X, I_Y, I_{xx}, I_{yy}, mag, o) \quad (2)$$
$$f_{color} = C(x, y, Ch_1, Ch_2, Ch_3) \quad (3)$$
$$f_{combination} = C(x, y, Ch_1, Ch_2, Ch_3, I_x, I_y, mag, o) \quad (4)$$

where Ch_x indicates the x color channel which is dependent on the used color space. mag and o are based on the first order derivatives with respect to x and y:

$$mag(x, y) = \sqrt{I_x^2(x, y) + I_y^2(x, y)} \quad (5)$$

$$o(x, y) = \arctan\left(\frac{I_y(x, y)}{I_x(x, y)}\right) \quad (6)$$

f_{shape} uses shape information in the form of I_x, I_y, I_{xx}, I_{yy}, mag and $order$ and no color information. f_{color} considers only color information while $f_{combination}$ uses a combination of both shape and color: All feature vectors are used as a collection of grids of region descriptors.

A second method to capture both shape and color information in a single descriptor is the use of color SIFT features. To obtain fixed-length feature vectors per image, the bag-of-words model is used [24], which is also known as 'textons' [18], 'object parts' [8] and 'codebooks' [13,17]. When using the bag-of-words model a large number of randomly sampled descriptors is clustered to obtain a visual codebook. In an image region all descriptors are then assigned to the codebook element which is closest in Euclidean space. To be independent of the total number of descriptors in an image, the feature vector is normalized to sum to 1. In this paper a visual codebook of 128 elements is constructed by applying k-means clustering to 20,000 randomly sampled descriptors from the set of images available for training. As descriptors we use both the traditional SIFT implementation without color information [19] and the concatenation of these descriptors calculated in each color channel separately.

3.2 Distance Metrics

To compare the resulting histogram features, several distance measures can be used, such as the Euclidean distance, intersection distance, quadratic cross distance and Bhattacharyya distance. Similar to [1] and [12] we use the Bhattacharyya distance:

$$D_{hist}(h_1, h_2) = -\ln\left(\sum_{x \in X} \sqrt{h_1(x) h_2(x)}\right) \quad (7)$$

This distance metric is unsuitable for measuring the distance between covariance matrices. So for comparing elements described using equation 1 we use the metric proposed by Forstner and Moonen [10] which sums the generalized eigenvalues of the covariances:

$$D_{covar}(C_1, C_2) = \sqrt{\sum_i \ln^2 \lambda_i(C_1, C_2)} \quad (8)$$

3.3 Invariant Descriptors

Changes in illumination and color of the light source can greatly affect matching results if the descriptors used are not robust to these changes. To make tracing robust to changes in shadows and shading, intensity invariance is needed. Various methods have been proposed to obtain invariance to these unwanted variations, where color models and color constancy focus on illumination and color respectively.

Color model. To measure colors of objects independent of shadings van de Sande et al. [26] studied two aspects of intensity invariance in a non-surveillance setting: light intensity change and light intensity shift. Light intensity change stands for the constant factor in all channels by which the image values change while light intensity shift stands for an equal shift in image intensity values in all channels. Similar to their overview we compare the following models:

RGB histogram. The RGB histogram is a 3-D histogram based on the R, G and B channels of the RGB color space. This histogram possesses no invariance properties and is the most basic representation.
Opponent histogram. The opponent histogram is a 3-D histogram based on the channels of the opponent color space YCbCr. This color space was designed to The color models of the first two channels are shift-invariant with respect to light intensity. The third channel possesses intensity information and has no invariance properties.
Hue histogram. The HSV histogram is a 3-D histogram based on the Hue, Saturation and Value channels of the HSV color space. The H and the S color models are scale-invariant and shift-invariant with respect to light intensity.
XYZ, Lab and Luv histogram. The XYZ, Lab and Luv histograms are 3-D histograms based on the XYZ, Lab and Luv colorspaces respectively. These colorspaces were designed to mimic the response of the human visual system.

Hue histogram and Opponent histogram can be used without the intensity channel. The Opponent histogram then becomes invariant to light intensity shift while the Hue histogram becomes invariant to intensity scale and shift. We aim for some level of intensity invariance, so normalized rgb, Hue histogram without intensity and Opponent histogram without intensity are expected to perform best for tracing.

Color constancy. Color constancy is the ability to measure colors of objects independent of the color of the light source [11]. For each video, frame or detection a correction is computed which virtually changes the color of the light source to white. For the RGB color space this leads to the following corrections:

$$R_{\text{output}} = \frac{R}{\sqrt{3} * R_{lightsource}} \tag{9}$$

$$G_{\text{output}} = \frac{G}{\sqrt{3} * G_{lightsource}} \tag{10}$$

$$B_{\text{output}} = \frac{B}{\sqrt{3} * B_{lightsource}} \tag{11}$$

where R, G and B are the input channels and $R_{lightsource}$, $G_{lightsource}$ and $B_{lightsource}$ are estimates of the light source. To estimate the light source the color constancy methods proposed by Forsyth [11] and Finlayson [9] are not applicable, due to their complex nature and dependency on calibration datasets. We therefore compare three methods to estimate the light source: Grey world [3], max-RGB [16] and Grey Edge [27].

Of the three models Grey edge is expected to perform best as Weijer et al. [27] showed that for real-world images color constancy based on the Grey-Edge hypothesis obtains better results than those obtained with the Grey-World method.

4 Experimental Results

In this section we assess the performance of the presented methods, color models and color constancy methods.

4.1 Evaluation Criteria

To assess the performance of the tracing methods, we consider two scenarios. The first is an investigator who wants to find clues to explore further. In this case it is important that some evidence of a person's presence in any camera is found. The second is the full reconstruction of the event where all instances of the person have to be found. In both scenarios there is an asymmetry between the camera used as starting point and other cameras. In the start camera the investigator can easily select the most appropriate detection to be used as query, and correct detections if needed. The detections in the other cameras cannot be controlled.

We resort to a method used for biometric identification systems that return ranked lists of candidates to express the performance of the proposed tracing methods: the Cumulative Matching Curve (CMC)[7]. Assuming we have a set of samples B_i with associated ground truth ID(B_i), two subsets of samples are created:

1. A *gallery* set G consisting of m samples of *different* subjects.
2. A *probe* set Q with n samples associated with the n subjects. The probe set Q can be from any set of individuals, but usually probe identities are presumed to be in the gallery G. The probe set may contain more than one sample of a given person and need not contain a sample of each subject in G.

In order to estimate the CMC, each probe sample is matched to every gallery sample resulting in a $n \times m$ similarity matrix S. The scores for each probe sample are ordered to assign a rank k to every gallery sample, where k_l is the rank of a gallery sample obtained from the same person as the probe sample. CMC(k) is then the fraction of probe samples that have rank $k_l \leq k$:

$$CMC(k) = \frac{1}{n}(\#k_l \leq k) \tag{12}$$

If an investigator is searching through a video archive it is unlikely that he or she is focused on finding all instances of that subject. It is more important that any instance of the subject in another camera is found as soon as possible as this might lead to more information about the subject. We therefore redefine the CMC curve. Again the scores for all probe samples are ordered to assign a rank k to every gallery sample, but for each query only the first match k_{first} is of importance. This metric is called the First Matching Curve or FMC. Formally, $FMC(k)$ is then the fraction of probe samples that have rank $k_{first} \leq k$:

$$FMC(k) = \frac{1}{n}(\#k_{first} \leq k) \tag{13}$$

4.2 Datasets

As benchmark we use the VIPeR dataset [12] to show the performance of all image matching techniques and invariance properties described in section 3. This dataset consists of 632 persons, where each person was photographed twice under various viewpoints, poses and lighting conditions. Sample pictures of this dataset are shown in figure 2. While the images in the VIPeR dataset are taken from surveillance cameras and a lot of variance is present, persons are always positioned in the center of the image and in an upward position.

In real-life, image matching techniques should not only be able to match these perfectly located persons, but also retrieve images of the same person with less than optimal detections. For that reason we recorded a dataset with the assistance of the Dutch police; twenty cameras are used without any overlap in

Fig. 2. Some examples of the VIPeR dataset

field-of-view. These recordings were made as part of the regular surveillance process for that area. A ground-truth is obtained by manually labeling the positions of four persons who were asked to walk around in the area under surveillance.

The dataset contains several sources of variation. Most notably are the presence of a large number of pedestrians participating in traffic, changes in weather, camera angle, colors and texture of clothing and reflections in windows. In addition, the area where we collected data was under active surveillance leading in some cases to movement of the cameras. Sample frames from this dataset are shown in figure 3.

Fig. 3. Sample frames of the used surveillance data

4.3 Results

The results are divided in two sections, we first present the performance on the VIPeR dataset and then show how the best method performs in an unconstrained situation.

Results on the VIPeR dataset. The average CMC curves on the VIPeR dataset can be found in figures 4, 5 and 6. Figure 4 shows that if a user is willing to observe the first 20 matches, in 70% of the cases the person he was looking for could be found.

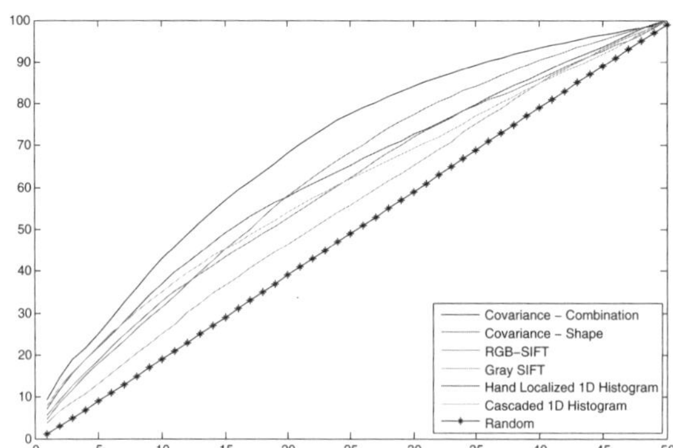

Fig. 4. CMC curves of the described matching techniques on the VIPeR dataset

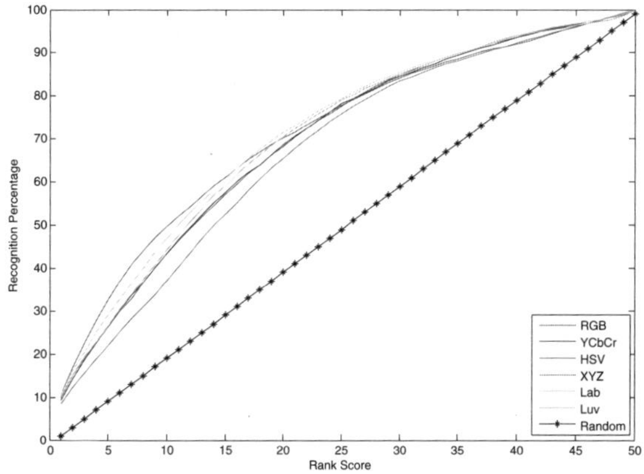

Fig. 5. CMC curves of color covariance matrix using different color spaces on the VIPeR dataset

To be able to compare different color constancy methods we apply the methods implemented by [27]. Similar to [27] we vary the order of the method, the Minkowski norm and the local smoothing. Specific parameter settings can be found in table 1.

Table 1. Parameter settings for different color constancy methods

Method	Parameters		
	Order	Minkowski	Smoothing
Grey-World	0	1	0
Max-RGB	0	∞	0
Shades of Grey	0	7	0
general Grey-World	0	11	1
Grey-Edge	1	7	4
2nd order Grey-Edge	2	7	5

In conclusion, the covariance matrix with both color and shape information performs best on this benchmark. Adding color constancy slightly improves results, with Max-RGB performing best. Different color models did not influence results greatly, but HSV slightly outperforms all other methods.

Results on the real-life dataset. Sample results of applying our person detection system to the real-life surveillance dataset are shown in figure 7. The detection results are thresholded in such a way that for each camera all persons in that camera's field-of-view were detected at least once. As a result, the number of false positives is large. Please note the large variation in amount of background within each bounding box.

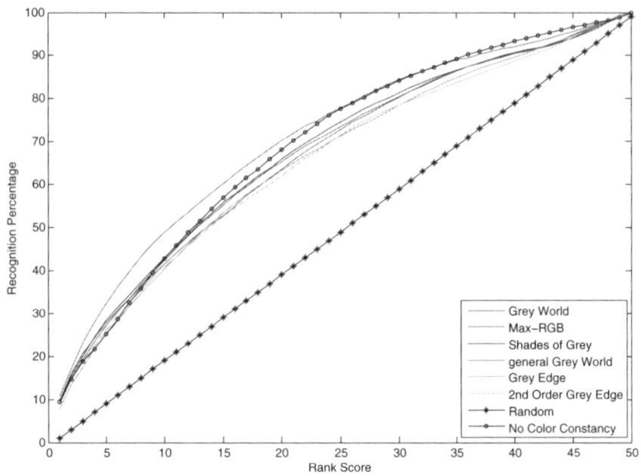

Fig. 6. CMC curves of color covariance matrix using different color constancy methods on the VIPeR dataset

Fig. 7. Sample frames of the used surveillance data with their detection results

The automatic detections generated by the person detection system described in section 2 were matched to the ground truth. All detections with an overlap larger than 75% with a ground truth region are labeled as that specific person. Elements in the ground-truth larger than 6000 pixels, showing a complete, unobstructed body and not over or under saturated are then used as queries. We order the automatic detections in other cameras based on similarity to the query. A selection of these queries is given in figure 8. Automatic detections with the same label as the query are considered a match. Sample orderings using Cascaded 1d Histograms and covariance matrices with a combination of color and shape features are given in figure 9.

For each person separately the average CMC curve is measured to show the influence of different clothing. Initially we use covariance matrices with the combination of color and shape information, Max-RGB color constancy and HSV color space since this method performed best on the VIPeR dataset. We use a binary, person shaped mask to reduce the influence of backgrounds. Results are shown in figure 10.

A clear difference in performance can be observed between the four subjects; when person one, two and three are used as queries approximately random

Fig. 8. The four persons used to query the automatic detections

Fig. 9. Sample orderings using Cascaded 1D Histograms (top row) and covariance matrices (bottom row). The query image is shown left with the first 7 results after the line.

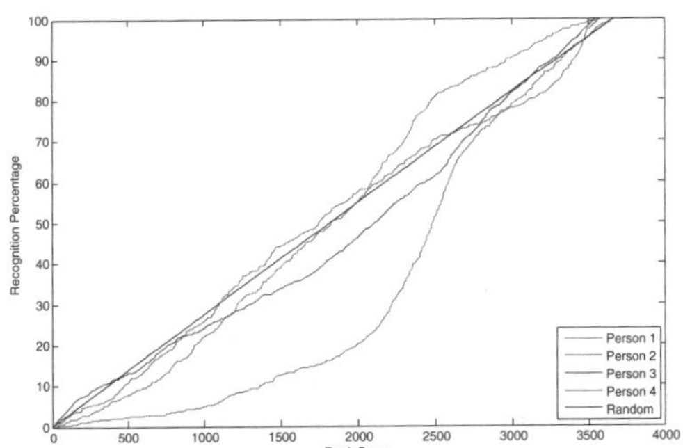

Fig. 10. CMC curves for different persons in real-life surveillance videos using Covariance matrices with a combination of shape and color information

performance is obtained. This means that if a person is to be found, it is in general better to search the dataset chronologically. For person four however, performance is much worse than random. Since this person is visually very distinctive by the red jacket, a direct conclusion is that a representation more focused on color is more suitable for this type of data.

Results of applying the Cascaded 1D Histogram are given in figure 11. Again Max-RGB color constancy is used, with the YCbCr colorspace and a binary,

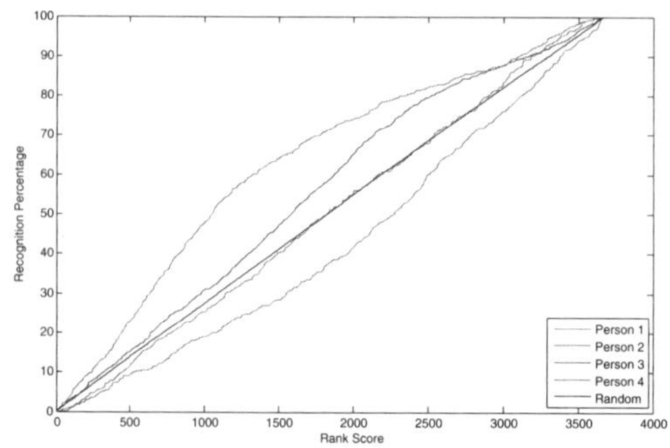

Fig. 11. CMC curves for different persons in real-life surveillance videos using Cascaded 1D Histograms

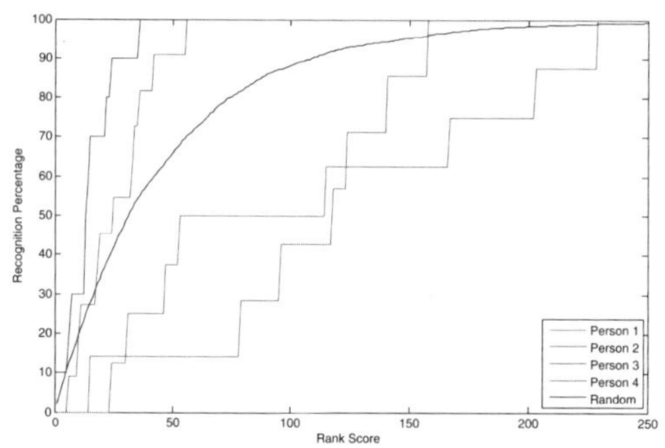

Fig. 12. FMC curves based on the first match for different person using Cascaded 1D Histograms. Only the first 250 ranks are shown out of 4000 image regions for readability.

person shaped mask. As expected, person four is retrieved more easily than the three other subjects. For person one the performance is similar to random which is mostly due to the large difference in back and frontal appearance. Person two appears to be more easily traced using covariance matrices than color histograms. This is due to the fact that this person wore mostly gray colored clothes while the pattern on the jacket is more distinctive. Lastly, while person three wore mostly black clothes the combination of the black jacket with the white shirt underneath proves to be a strong enough visual cue to be able to trace ths person. In situation where the shirt was not visible it is unfeasible to find this person.

As mentioned earlier a person using the described person tracing system might not be interested in finding all instances of the person he or she is looking for but is more interested in finding a single instance of that person in another camera as fast as possible. We therefore apply the FMC metric to the same data and method. We show the results in figure 12.

The same observations we made after figure 11 apply here, but now the best results are obtained for person three instead of person four. The reason for this is that the image regions where for person three both his jacket and shirt were visible had a very high ranking. A user of a tracing system as described in this paper would then be able to obtain extra information leading to easier searches for other instances.

5 Conclusion

In this paper we showed various methods to describe an image region which were used to trace a person over multiple cameras. We showed that a combination of color and shape information is needed for effective tracing on a dataset simulating perfect detection results. In situations where the detections are not so good however, this combination proved unsuccessful. A method focusing solely on color information was effective for two of the four subjects. This leads to the conclusion that before searching for a particular person the defining characteristics should be determined. If that person is wearing black clothes, any color based feature representation will fail for its inability to represent the color distribution properly. In these cases either more information should be used or a simple chronological search is recommended. If, however, the subject wears clothes with one or more distinctive colors, enough visual cues are present to be able to search through all videos based on a color-based feature representation.

To deal with changes in light and shadings, various color models and color constancy methods were applied. We showed that color constancy can slightly improve results by reducing the influence of color changes between cameras. Secondly, the use of a color space invariant to intensity is shown to improve tracing results by reducing the influence of shades.

We would like to point out that instead of using a single image of a person as query, multiple detections of the same person can be combined to obtain a track representation. Since such a representation can combine spatial and temporal information with the appearance information used in this paper, tracing performance could be greatly improved. Another point of interest is the large number of background regions falsely classified as persons. This issue can be dealt with in two ways. First of all the background extraction method can be improved. Background extraction is a very challenging task, but great results have been achieved. However, there is still enough room for improvement. Secondly, the model classifying regions of interest as pedestrians can be improved. We described a method which is generally considered the state-of-the-art in person detection, but the SVM classifier was trained on a general pedestrian dataset. We expect a big improvement by training the model on a dataset more focused on real-life surveillance data.

In conclusion, methods for automating the process of incident reconstruction are promising, but it is a major step from the lab to real-life surveillance data. Our results give some guidelines for optimizing the process and for seeing under which conditions automatic analysis should be pursued.

References

1. Alahi, A., Vandergheynst, P., Bierlaire, M., Kunt, M.: Cascade of descriptors to detect and track objects across any network of cameras. Preprint submitted to Computer Vision and Image Understanding (2009)
2. Black, J., Ellis, T.: Multi camera image tracking. Image Vision Comput. 24(11), 1256–1267 (2006)
3. Buchsbaum, G.: A spatial processor model for object colour perception. Journal of the Franklin Institute 310(1), 337–350 (1980)
4. Calderara, S., Prati, A., Cucchiara, R.: Hecol: Homography and epipolar-based consistent labeling for outdoor park surveillance. Computer Vision and Image Understanding 111(1), 21–42 (2008)
5. Dalal, N., Triggs, B.: Histograms of oriented gradients for human detection. In: CVPR 2005: Proceedings of the 2005 IEEE Computer Society Conference on Computer Vision and Pattern Recognition, vol. 2, pp. 886–893 (2005)
6. Datcu, D., Yang, Z., Rothkrantz, L.: Multimodal workbench for automatic surveillance applications. In: IEEE Computer Society Conference on Computer Vision and Pattern Recognition, vol. 0, pp. 1–2 (2007)
7. Dunstone, T., Yager, N.: Biometric System and Data Analysis: Design, Evaluation, and Data Mining. Springer Publishing Company, Incorporated, Heidelberg (2008)
8. Fergus, R., Perona, P., Zisserman, A.: Object class recognition by unsupervised scale-invariant learning. In: IEEE Computer Society Conference on Computer Vision and Pattern Recognition, vol. 2, pp. 264–271 (2003)
9. Finlayson, G., Hordley, S.: Gamut constrained illumination estimation. International Journal of Computer Vision 67(1), 93–109 (2006)
10. Forstner, W., Moonen, B.: A metric for covariance matrices. Qua vadis geodesia 1, 113–128 (1999)
11. Forsyth, D.: A novel algorithm for color constancy. International Journal of Computer Vision 5(1), 5–36 (1990)
12. Gray, D., Brennan, S., Tao, H.: Evaluating appearance models for recognition, reacquisition, and tracking. In: Performance Evaluation of Tracking and Surveillance, PETS (2007)
13. Jurie, F., Triggs, B.: Creating efficient codebooks for visual recognition. In: ICCV 2005: Proceedings of the Tenth IEEE International Conference on Computer Vision (ICCV 2005), Washington, DC, USA, vol. 1, pp. 604–610. IEEE Computer Society, Los Alamitos (2005)
14. Kalman, R.: A new approach to linear filtering and prediction problems. Journal of Basic Engineering 82(1), 35–45 (1960)
15. Koppen, P., Worring, M.: Multi-target tracking in time-lapse video forensics. In: MiFor 2009: Proceedings of the First ACM workshop on Multimedia in forensics, pp. 61–66. ACM, New York (2009)
16. Land, E., McCann, J.: Lightness and retinex theory. The Journal of the Optical Society of America A 61(1), 1–11 (1971)
17. Leibe, B., Schiele, B.: Interleaved object categorization and segmentation. In: British Machine Vision Conference, pp. 759–768 (2003)
18. Leung, T., Malik, J.: Representing and recognizing the visual appearance of materials using three-dimensional textons. Int. J. Comput. Vision 43(1), 29–44 (2001)
19. Lowe, D.: Distinctive image features from scale-invariant keypoints. International Journal of Computer Vision 20, 91–110 (2003)

20. Nowak, E., Jurie, F.: Learning visual similarity measures for comparing never seen objects. Computer Vision and Pattern Recognition 1, 1–8 (2007)
21. Pham, T., Worring, M., Smeulders, A.: A multi-camera visual surveillance system for tracking of reoccurences of people. In: International Conference on Distributed Smart Cameras, vol. 1, pp. 164–169 (2007)
22. Piciarelli, C., Micheloni, C., Foresti, G.: Trajectory-based anomalous event detection 18(11), 1544–1554 (2008)
23. Rao, C., Ray, A., Sarkar, S., Yasar, M.: Review and comparative evaluation of symbolic dynamic filtering for detection of anomaly patterns 3(2) (2009)
24. Sivic, J., Zisserman, A.: Video google: A text retrieval approach to object matching in videos. In: IEEE International Conference on Computer Vision, vol. 2, p. 1470 (2003)
25. Tuzel, O., Porikli, F., Meer, P.: Region covariance: A fast descriptor for detection and classification. In: Leonardis, A., Bischof, H., Pinz, A. (eds.) ECCV 2006. LNCS, vol. 3952, pp. 589–600. Springer, Heidelberg (2006)
26. van de Sande, K.E.A., Gevers, T., Snoek, C.G.M.: Evaluation of color descriptors for object and scene recognition. In: IEEE Conference on Computer Vision and Pattern Recognition, Anchorage, Alaska, USA (2008)
27. van de Weijer, J., Gevers, T., Gijsenij, A.: Edge-based color constancy. IEEE Transactions on Image Processing 16(9), 2207–2214 (2007)
28. Vapnik, V.N.: The nature of statistical learning theory. Springer, New York (1995)
29. Yilmaz, A., Javed, O., Shah, M.: Object tracking: A survey. ACM Comput. Surv. 38(4), 13 (2006)
30. Zajdel, W., Krijnders, J.D., Andringa, T., Gavrila, D.M.: Cassandra: Audio-video sensor fusion for aggression detection. In: IEEE Int. Conf. on Advanced Video and Signal based Surveillance, AVSS (2007)
31. Zhou, Q., Aggarwal, J.K.: Object tracking in an outdoor environment using fusion of features and cameras. Image Vision Comput. 24(11), 1244–1255 (2006)
32. Zivkovic, Z., der Heijden, F.: Efficient adaptive density estimation per image pixel for the task of background subtraction. Pattern Recognition Letters 27, 773–780 (2006)

Collusion-Resistant Fingerprinting Systems: Review and Recent Results

Byung-Ho Cha and C.-C. Jay Kuo

Ming-Hsieh Department of Electrical Engineering
University of Southern California, Los Angeles, CA 90089-2564
byungcha@usc.edu, cckuo@sipi.usc.edu

Abstract. This paper provides a review of previous work and recent results on the design and analysis of collusion-resistant fingerprinting systems. Collusion attacks examined in previous work are with constant weights for all colluders. Collusion attacks on continuous media (such as audio and video) with time-varying weights are simple to implement, but have never been treated by other researchers. In recent years, we have proposed a new fingerprinting system called MC-CDMA-based fingerprinting since it is inspired by the multi-carrier code division multi-access (MC-CDMA) communication technique. The time-varying collusion attack can be conveniently analyzed by drawing an analogy to the multi-access interference (MAI) problem in a wireless communication system with a time-varying channel response. As a result, many powerful tools from wireless communications can be borrowed to design a collusion-resistant fingerprinting system. They include codeword design, shifted spreading, pilot-based channel estimation, receiver design, etc. Furthermore, we present results on capacity, throughput, and distortion of a colluded media file. Finally, we will mention some open research problems.

Keywords: multi-access interference, time-varying collusion attacks, human perceptual system, multimedia distortion, advanced detection, collusion-resistant fingerprinting.

1 Introduction

Fingerprinting technology provides a solution to traitor tracing in multimedia distribution over the Internet. One powerful scheme to break the fingerprint-based traitor tracing system is the collusion attacks [1, 2, 3]. Users that have the same content but different embedding codes may merge their received copies via linear combination with an attempt to remove their individual codes without degrading media quality much. When the attack is successful, the traitor tracing system will not be able to identify participating attackers from this newly generated copy. The design and analysis of collusion-resistant fingerprinting system has been an important research topic for years.

Despite these research efforts, fingerprinting research still remains in the context of storage data protection and static attacks from attackers [4]. The concept

Y.Q. Shi (Ed.): Transactions on DHMS V, LNCS 6010, pp. 34–50, 2010.

of fingerprinting applications was originated from a bit-stream protection for database management. In this scenario, to insert bit errors in a bit-stream was the best way to break a fingerprinting system. Thus, most previous fingerprinting research deals with collusion attacks with equal weights or its variants (*e.g.*, the cascade of several collusion attacks with equal weights). Consequently, the weight of each colluder is a constant throughout the collusion process. However, the collusion attack on continuous media such as audio and video with time-varying weights is simple to implement. Since techniques developed in the past fail to provide a satisfactory solution to time-varying attacks, a new solution framework is needed.

In recent years, a sequence of papers have been published by authors [5,6,7,8, 9,10,11] for such a new framework. The resultant fingerprinting system is called MC-CDMA-based fingerprinting since it was inspired by the multi-carrier code division multi-access (MC-CDMA) communication system. The time-varying collusion attack can be conveniently analyzed by drawing an analogy to the multi-access interference (MAI) problem in a wireless communication system with a time-varying channel response. Furthermore, many powerful tools from wireless communications can be borrowed to design a collusion-resistant fingerprint system. They include codeword design, shifted spreading, pilot-based channel estimation, receiver design, etc.

After the review of the MC-CDMA fingerprinting system, we mention some remaining research issues. The physical channel in a wireless communication setting is controlled by the environment, which is often modeled by a norm-bounded quasi-stationary random process. Coherence usually remains during a short period of time. However, these properties can be violated by time-varying collusion attacks. To shed some light along this direction, we discuss recent results of our work on capacity, throughput, and distortion of a colluded media file. We will mention some open research problems and challenges. Finally, concluding remarks are given.

2 Review of Previous Work

2.1 Coalition and Collusion Attacks

Coalition attacks are usually discussed in the context of digital fingerprinting for the tracing of the header file and/or the secret key alternation. An example of the coalition attack is illustrated in Fig. 1. The coalition attack assumes bit errors in the fingerprint code, and if the fingerprint code is not properly designed, the distinction of each fingerprint code disappears. Thus, the system loses its ability to separate fingerprint codes of colluders from others. This problem can be solved by combinatorial design and coding theory [4] under the assumption that each fingerprint code experiences independent bit alterations.

In contrast, collusion attacks are usually considered in the context of multimedia fingerprinting. An example of the collusion attack is illustrated in Fig. 2.

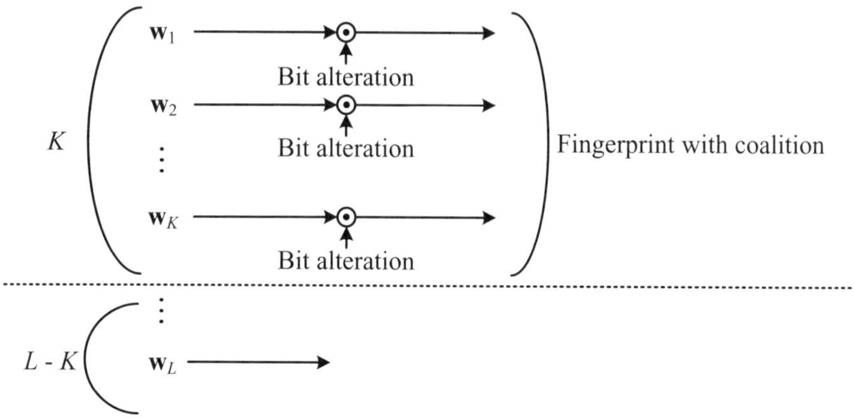

Fig. 1. Illustration of a coalition attack

The collusion attack is simply implemented by applying weights to the fingerprinted media. Colluders must normalize the sum of all weights to one so as to preserve the media quality after the collusion attack is applied. The collusion attack often assumes a fairness condition in the sense that all colluders share their risk equally.

There are some extended collusion attacks. For example, Stone [1] proposed a weighted collusion attack using random coefficients, which is called the jamming attack in [2]. Two types of collusion attacks are investigated in the media fingerprinting literature, *i.e.*, linear and nonlinear collusion attacks [3], as the extension of Stone's observations.

Linear collusion attacks have been studied extensively. In the average collusion attack, weights of all users are set to equal to meet the fairness condition among colluders. However, the fairness condition is only meaningful with respect to correlation detection with equal power fingerprints in the statistical sense [12], [13]. Since there may exist selfish colluders who would like to minimize their risk, the pre-colluded collusion attack was considered in [14]. That is, colluders are divided into several groups, and an average collusion attack is first performed in each individual group. Then, another average collusion attack is performed on the outputs of all groups. The average and pre-colluded collusion attacks are both special cases of a weighted collusion attack.

Results on nonlinear collusion attacks are relatively fewer. It was shown in [15, 3, 12] that nonlinear collusion attacks do not offer any advantage over the average collusion attacks in terms of colluded multimedia quality. It was claimed in [16] that all manipulations of nonlinear collusion attacks can be explained by linear collusion attacks with noise.

Despite the research efforts mentioned above, there exists an effective collusion attack which has however been overlooked in the past; namely, time-varying

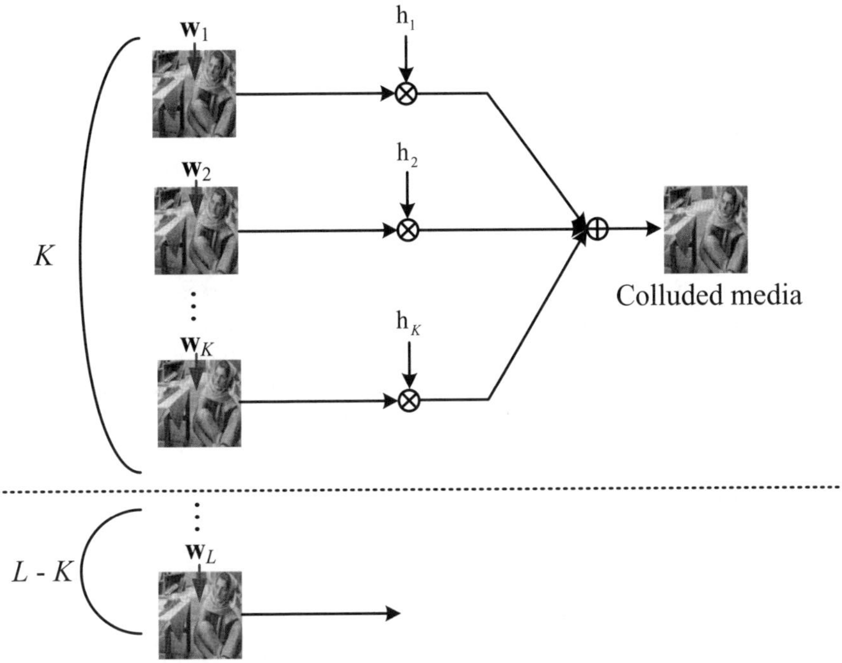

Fig. 2. Illustration of a collusion attack

weighted (or dynamic) collusion attacks applied to continuous media such as audio and video. It is easy to design a time-varying attack which still meets the fairness condition over time. That is, we may rotate colluders with larger weights along time so that their time-average is still the same. Unfortunately, solutions developed for static collusion attacks do not work well for dynamic collusion attacks. It demands a new framework for solution.

2.2 Coalition-Resistant Fingerprinting

Combinatorial design is methodology to design codes defined by finite sets whose interconnections meet some specified numerical relationship. Combinatorial design is closely related to the generation of codes for fingerprinting applications. Fundamental combinatorial codes and their relationships are well reviewed in [17]. These fingerprint codes are created to protect generic data such as softwares, text data, or bitstreams.

Fingerprinting with tracing capability was originated from Wagner *et al.* [18], and fingerprinting resilient against pirate coalitions was studied by Blakley *et al.* [4] in the 80s. The identifiable parent property (IPP) codes [19] were developed to deal with two pirate users. A concept of frame-proof (FP) codes under the marking assumption was introduced by Boneh and Shaw in [20]. To design a specific code that resists the collusion attack, they proposed a collusion-secure (CS) code based on a marking assumption. Their method can catch one out of c colluders with a high probability if these colluders are not able to change the state of undetectable marks. However, their method has some limitations. First, it works well only for symbol sequences but not multimedia data, since the latter can be manipulated through noise and re-quantization. Second, the code length is very long for a large value of c because it is proportional to $c^4 log^2 L$ to support a total number of L users. As an extension of CS codes, the traceability (TA) codes [21] were developed by several researchers to increase tracing capabilities against coalition attacks. More recently, optimal randomized fingerprint codes were proposed by Tardos [22]. His fingerprint codes achieved the same performance as CS codes but with a shorter code length, $c^2 logL$, to support L users when the marking assumption holds.

2.3 Collusion-Resistant Fingerprinting

A series of research has been done in the last decade to deal with the threat of collusion attacks. Collusion-resistant fingerprinting can be categorized into two classes [23, 3]: independent fingerprinting and coded fingerprinting. For independent fingerprinting, Cox *et al.* [24] proposed a spread spectrum (SS) watermark generation and embedding technique, where codes are generated randomly by an independently identically distributed (i.i.d.) uniform or Gaussian source. It was shown experimentally that the resulting codes are robust against average collusion attacks to a certain degree. However, no quantitative analysis was provided.

Wang *et al.* [16] investigated the error performance of pseudo-noise (PN) codes using maximum and threshold detectors, and she proposed a method to estimate the size of colluders. Zhao *et al.* [15] conducted a forensic analysis for unbounded Gaussian (UG) and bounded Gaussian (BG) codes under non-linear collusion attacks (*e.g.*, max, min, and median operations). Research in [16] and [15] gave a thorough performance analysis on the relationship among the code length and the user and colluder number, and it derived lower and upper bounds on probability error functions with respect to specific collusion attack models. Recently, a new scheme was proposed by Li and Trappe [25] based on the concept of the Welch bounded equality (WBE) and the sphere decoding method.

Coded fingerprinting, which integrates watermarking technique with combinatorial and coding theory, was first introduced by Yacobi [2]. Along this research direction, Trappe *et al.* [26] proposed a scheme called AND-anti-collusion-codes (AND-ACC) using the orthogonal code modulation. AND-ACC requires shorter codewords and achieves better colluder identification performance than the CS code. He and Wu [27] extended the CS code to the traceability (TA) codes using the spread spectrum modulation (SSM) and a cross-layer design that separates coding and modulation.

3 MC-CDMA-Based Fingerprinting and Time-Varying Collusion Attacks

3.1 System Overview

Consider that colluders change their colluder weights from time to time in the collusion process of continuous media. To trace the dynamic nature of time-varying collusion attacks, we may draw an analogy between the fingerprinting system and the multiuser communication system. We claim that the collusion-resistant fingerprinting problem can be viewed as the symbol detection problem in a multi-carrier code-division-multi-access (MC-CDMA) communication system.

There are several ways to allow multiple users to access to a shared channel, *e.g.*, TDMA (time-division multi-access), FDMA (frequency-division multi-access), CDMA (code-division multi-access), MC-CDMA (multi-carrier code-division multi-access) and OFDMA (orthogonal frequency division multi-access) [28]. One goal of a wireless multi-access communication system is to accommodate as many users as possible in a shared channel of finite capacity while meeting certain detection performance.

To reduce the interference caused by multi-user access, known as the multiple access interference (MAI), in wireless communications, Tsai *et al.* [29, 30] proposed to use the Hadamard-Walsh codes as spreading codes in MC-CDMA systems. It was shown in [5, 6] that the same design can be used to obtain collusion-resistant fingerprints. Furthermore, we introduced the delayed embedding idea in [7, 8] to increase the user capacity. That is, a codeword can be circularly shifted to generate new codewords for other users. When these codewords are colluded, this is equivalent to a multi-path fading channel. Finally, to improve fingerprint detection performance, several advanced symbol detection schemes were discussed in [9, 10, 11].

In this section, we review the MC-CDMA-based fingerprinting system proposed in [9, 10, 11]. As shown in Fig. 3, it consists of three modules: 1) the fingerprint generation and embedding module, 2) the time-varying collusion attack module, and 3) the fingerprint detection module. They are detailed below.

3.2 Fingerprint Generation and Embedding

Let Φ be the user set and $|\Phi| = L$ the user number. The user message, m_l, of length M contains user identification (ID) u_l of length U and error correction codes of length $M - U$. Furthermore, $s_l(i)$ denotes the spreading code where i represents time or spatial sample index. Then, the user code, $w_l(i)$, is obtained via

$$w_l(i) = \mathrm{IDFT}\{m_l s_l(i)\} \tag{1}$$

where the IDFT is the inverse discrete Fourier transform. The number of users is decided by units of spreading codes. If we use $N \times N$ Hadamard-Walsh (HW) codes or $N \times N$ carrier interferometry (CI) codes, they can support N users [9].

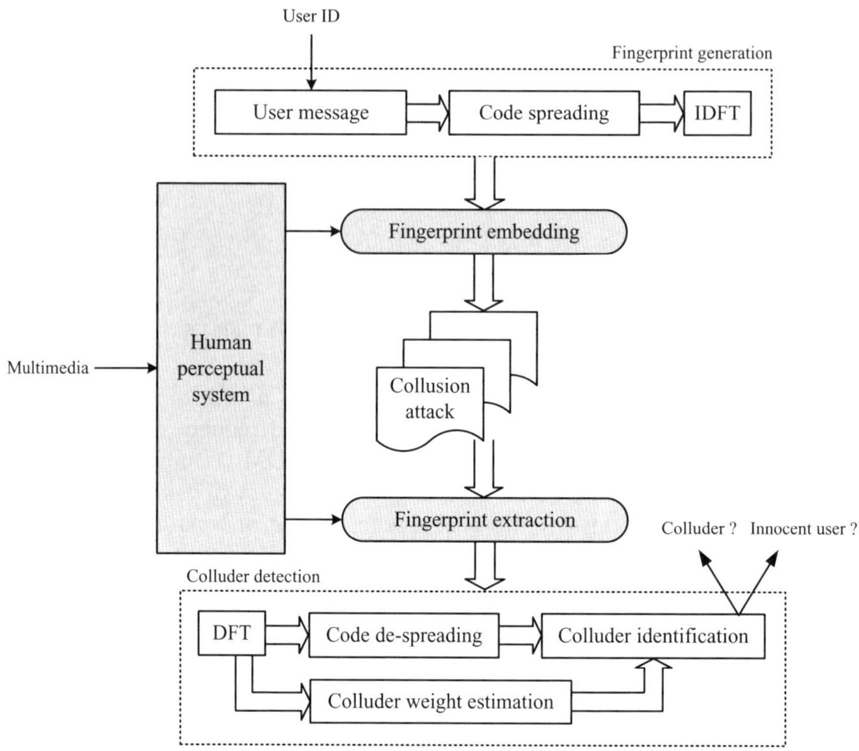

Fig. 3. The block-diagram of the overall system with three modules: 1) fingerprint generation and embedding, 2) time-varying collusion attack, and 3) fingerprint detection

In code embedding, let $x_l(i)$, $i = 0, \cdots, T-1$, be selected discrete cosine transform (DCT) coefficients for user l according to the human visual system (HVS). We divide this set into B segments, each of which has N samples, as

$$x_l(i) = x_l(b \cdot N + n), \quad \begin{cases} b = 0 \ \cdots \ B-1 \\ n = 0 \ \cdots \ N-1 \end{cases}. \tag{2}$$

The additive code embedding method with shifted spreading [7] is given mathematically by

$$y_l(i - \Delta_l) = x_l(i - \Delta_l) + a_l(i - \Delta_l) \tag{3}$$

where

$$a_l(i - \Delta_l) = \alpha(i) w_l(i), \tag{4}$$

and where Δ_l is a shift amount under condition $P << N$ and $\alpha(i)$ is the embedded code strength, which is adaptively decided by the human perceptual model given in Sec. 4. By shifted spreading, we are able to increase the user number from N to $P \times N$.

Specifically, we consider a fingerprint code of $B_m B_n$ bits, where B_m bits are used as the user message and B_n bits are used for spreading codes. Since each user is assigned one out of $2^{(B_m-1)}$ ID numbers and one out of B_n spreading codeword, the user capacity is $2^{(B_m-1)}B_n$. To accommodate an even larger number of users, we propose a shifted spreading scheme that shifts the spreading codeword circularly by a certain amount. By allowing B_p-bit shifts (with $B_p < N-1$), the number of users increases from $2^{(B_m-1)}B_n$ to $2^{(B_m-1)}B_n(B_p+1)$ [8,11].

3.3 Time-Varying Collusion Attack

We divide users into two groups: malicious users (or colluders) and innocent users, and use Ω to denote the set of colluders. Clearly, Ω is a subset of Φ. Without loss of generality, we assume that there are L users and K colluders in the system. That is, $|\Phi| = L$ and $|\Omega| = K$. A time-varying collusion attack can be expressed as

$$\hat{y}(i) = \sum_{k\in\Omega} h_k(i) y_k(i) + e(i) \tag{5}$$

where $y_k(i)$ is the host signal, $h_k(i)$ the time-varying weight for colluder k, $e(i)$ additive noise and $\hat{y}(i)$ the colluded signal on the ith sample. The weights should satisfy the following condition:

$$\sum_{k\in\Omega} h_k(i) = 1 \tag{6}$$

where $h_k(i) \neq 0$ for all i. Furthermore, colluders can change their colluder weights arbitrarily without the knowledge of embedding and detection algorithms. We express the value of $h_k(i)$ as

$$h_k(i) = \tilde{h}_k(r;q), \quad r = 0, \cdots, R(q)-1 \quad \text{and} \quad q = 1, \cdots, Q \tag{7}$$

where $R(q)$ represents the number of samples in segment q, which varies in each segment, and Q represents the number of segments in one media.

3.4 Fingerprint Extraction and Colluder Identification

We extract fingerprint codes from the host media via

$$\hat{y}(i) - x(i) = \sum_{l\in\Phi} h_l(i)\hat{w}_l(i) + (\alpha(i))^{-1} e(i). \tag{8}$$

After the extraction, the discrete Fourier transform (DFT) is taken before user detection:

$$\sum_{l\in\Phi} m_l \lambda_l(i) \hat{s}_l(i) = \text{DFT}\left\{ \sum_{l\in\Phi} h_l(i)\hat{w}_l(i) + \tilde{e}(i) \right\} \tag{9}$$

where $\tilde{e}(i) = (\alpha(i))^{-1} e(i)$. Then, user detection, which includes synchronization, colluder weight estimation, and group/subgroup ID identification with threshold τ, is performed by advanced detectors.

When L users are supported, L user detection steps must be performed. Let $\hat{u}_l$ be the user ID decoded from detected message $\hat{m}_l$. Colluders can be distinguished from innocent users by a colluder identification process based on the following principle:

- $\Pr[\hat{u}_k \neq u_k] \rightarrow 0$ for colluder set Ω; and
- $\Pr[\hat{u}_j = u_j] \rightarrow 0$ for innocent user set Γ.

Specific decision rules can be derived accordingly.

The colluder weights $h_l(i)$ can be estimated by the detector. A detector must have some knowledge of colluder weights in order to apply advanced symbol detection techniques. The task of determining colluders' attack weights can be formulated as a channel estimation problem, which arises in a wireless communication system. There are several existing solutions to this problem [31, 32]. The pilot-aided estimation technique is often used in practice due to its simplicity. To improve the performance of colluder detection, the maximum ratio combining (MRC) and the multiuser detector (MUD) techniques can be used in association with pilot-aided estimation [33, 34]. For more details on this topic, we refer to [11].

4 Recent Results on Capacity/Throughput/Quality Analysis

Commercial audio and video contents have a length from 4-5 minutes in a music file to several hours in a movie file. We would like to answer the following questions:

1. What is the largest number of users to be supported in a host media?
2. What is the maximum number of colluders that can be detected?
3. Can we characterize the distortion of a colluded file based on the number of colluders and their weights?

They are still on-going research topics. In this section, we would like to provide some preliminary results for these interesting yet challenging problems.

4.1 Capacity Analysis

The embedding rate of a host media can be estimated from the human perceptual system model, which has been studied in [35, 36, 37, 38, 39]. Empirically, the embedding rate for a typical music and movie content is approximately 0.04 bits per sample. This value can be calculated from the imperceptibility criterion based on the perceptual masking threshold for audio [39, 40] and video [37, 38].

Fig. 4 shows the relationship between the maximum allowed power for imperceptible distortion from the human perceptual system model P_J, the fingerprint power P_F, the interference power P_I, and the noise power P_N. Here, i represents time or spatial sample index.

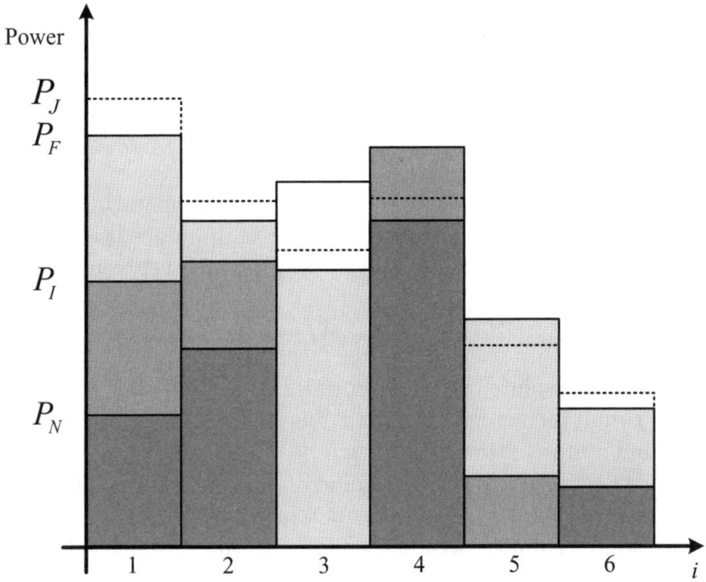

Fig. 4. Relationship between the maximum allowed power from the human perceptual system model P_J, fingerprint power P_F, interference power P_I, and noise power P_N

1. For fingerprint embedding with imperceptibility, we demand

$$P_F(i) \leq P_J(i). \tag{10}$$

2. For multimedia imperceptibility, we demand

$$P_F(i) + P_I(i) + P_N(i) \leq P_J(i). \tag{11}$$

3. For fingerprint identification, we demand

$$P_F(i) > P_I(i) + P_N(i). \tag{12}$$

For fingerprint embedding, It is desirable to have $P_F = P_J$ in Eq. (10) since colluders should also choose attacks which satisfy Eq. (11) for distortion imperceptibility. However, colluders should keep Eq. (12) in mind to break their fingerprint codes. Condition 1) is violated at sample position $i = 3$. Condition 2) is violated at sample positions $i = 4$ and 5. Condition 3) is violated at sample position $i = 1$, 2, and 4. Thus, only sample position $i = 6$ meets all three requirements stated above.

We provide an example in the audio fingerprinting application. Under the assumption $P_F = P_J$, we consider a short-time Fourier transform (STFT) domain audio embedding scheme given by [41, 42]

$$F_\theta(w) = \sum_{i=-\infty}^{\infty} f(i)w(i - \theta R) \exp(-jwi), \tag{13}$$

where $w(i)$ is a Hanning window of length θ and R is a hop size. Note that $w(i)$ should meet the following constant overlap-add (COLA) property:

$$\sum_{\theta=-\infty}^{\infty} w(i - \theta R) = 1. \tag{14}$$

Every windowed sample is selected by the masking operation of the human auditory system (HAS) model. Only unmasked samples are used for fingerprint embedding. Overall masking is decided by $Z(f)$, which is given by

$$Z(f) = \max\left(Z_m(f),\ Z_q(f)\right), \tag{15}$$

where $Z_q(f)$ is the absolute threshold pure-tone masking, $Z_m(f)$ is the absolute threshold for simultaneous masking, and f is in the unit of kHz. The details of the experiments and resulting weights can be found in [40].

In the above discussion, P_J is determined by the masking $Z(f)$ while P_I and P_N are selected by colluders. P_I is closely related with the number of colluders and the selection of colluder weights, and P_N is often influenced by additional signal processing effects (*e.g.*, noise, quantization, and filtering). P_I and P_N cannot be controlled by the fingerprinting embedder and detector. However, their values can be measured by the fingerprinting detector, and their strength has to be constrained by the colluded media distortion to be described in following two subsections.

4.2 Throughput Analysis

We may define the following two concepts related to throughput:

- Instantaneous throughput $\mathbb{T}_{ins}(t)$
  It is determined by the fingerprint power and the strength of collusion attacks at a given time interval centered around t. The strength of collusion attacks is determined by the number of colluders participating in collusion attacks and the selection of colluder weights.
- Total throughput $\mathbb{T}_{tot}$
  It is the summation of all instantaneous throughput over the entire continuous host media.

Lower throughput means that we receive fewer messages of the kth colluder and, as a result, it will be more difficult to perform accurate detection. This relationship can be analyzed below.

Let us consider a time interval: $(t_1, t_2]$. On one hand, the capacity of the host media in this interval is equal to $\mathbb{R}_E \times (t_2 - t_1)$, which is governed by JND. On the other hand, the colluder throughput $\mathbb{T}_{tot,k}$ in the same interval can be written as

$$\mathbb{T}_{tot,k}(t_1, t_2) = \int_{t_1}^{t_2} \mathbb{T}_{ins,k}(t)dt. \tag{16}$$

The averaged throughput is equal to the total throughput divided by the number of colluders, K. It can be written mathematically as

$$\mathbb{T}_{ave,k}(t_1, t_2) = \frac{\mathbb{T}_{tot,k}(t_1, t_2)}{K}, \tag{17}$$

The average detection probability of a colluder is related to the average throughput. The higher the average throughput, the higher the average detection probability. The characterization between the average throughput and the average detection probability also depends on the detector design.

One way to get the bound of instantaneous throughput is to use the information-theoretic capacity. The classic information-theoretic capacity region for colluders with white Gaussian noise $e(i)$ in the Gaussian multiple-access channel (GMAC) can be written as

$$\sum_{k \in \Omega} \mathbb{R}_k < \frac{1}{2} \log\left(1 + \zeta_{FNR}\right), \tag{18}$$

which is in the unit of bits per message symbol [43]. Here, ζ_{FNR} where FNR stands for fingerprint-to-noise ratio is given by

$$\zeta_{FNR} = \frac{\sum_{k \in \Omega} \sum_{n=0}^{N-1} |\lambda_k(n)|^2 p_{F,k}(n)}{N\sigma^2}, \tag{19}$$

where Eq. (19) can be derived from Eq. (9), $p_{F,k}$ is the fingerprint power for the kth colluder, and σ is the standard deviation of noise component $e(i)$. Eq. (18) represents the maximum sum rate to be achieved by the total power of colluders in Ω without interactions among colluders. It can be used to represent the rough upper bound of instantaneous throughput $\mathbb{T}_{ins,k}(t)$. For more details, we refer to [33, 28].

The number of colluders, K, should be known to calculate the average throughput. In practice, the fingerprinting detector estimates the number of colluders. This task is closely related to the user identification in communication. The accuracy of estimate the number of colluders, K, affects the performance of the fingerprinting detector.

4.3 Distortion of Colluded Media

We may classify time-varying collusion attacks into three types: 1) the segment-wise constant collusion attack, 2) the slow time-varying collusion attack, and 3) the fast time-varying collusion attack. We use the coherent time to denote the changing speed of weights in a time-varying collusion attack. Generally speaking, the shorter the coherent time, the poorer the colluder detection performance.

Another challenge may arise as illustrated in Fig. 5, where the colluder weights of time-varying collusion attack change with a wider dynamic range over a short period of time. It is well known in communication that channel coefficients with

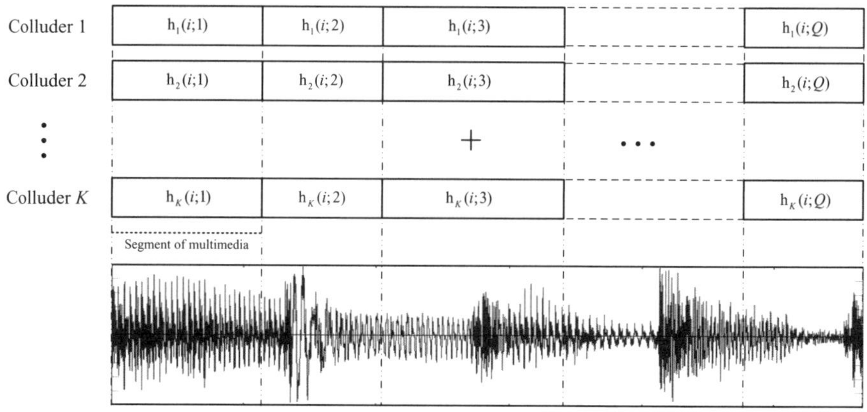

Fig. 5. Time-varying collusion attacks with a large dynamic range over a short period of time in a media file

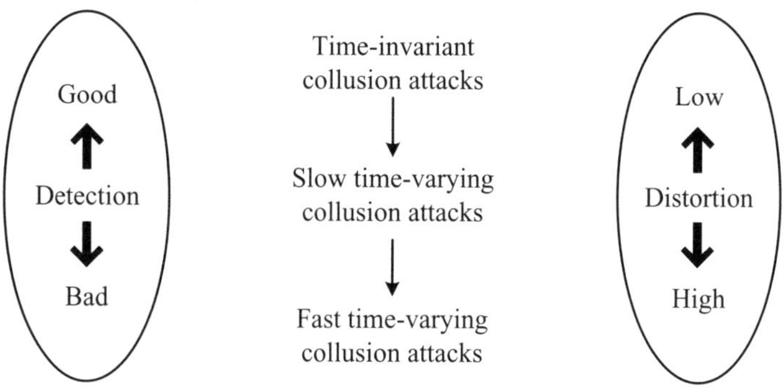

Fig. 6. Tradeoff between the colluder detection performance and the colluded image quality and their dependence on the coherent time

a lager dynamic range complicates the task of user detection [28]. Degraded user detection performance is closely related to impairments of colluder weight estimation (CWE) due to the large dynamic range of colluder weights.

The number of colluders and the coherent time determine the quality of a colluded media file. This relationship has been investigated for image, audio, and video by the authors. A qualitative characterization of the tradeoff between the colluder detection performance and colluded image quality is depicted in Fig. 6. That is, when the coherent time is shorter, the colluder detection performance becomes poorer while the distortion of the colluded media becomes higher. As a result, there is a bound on the maximum colluder number and the minimum coherent time due to the quality consideration. We may relate the coherent

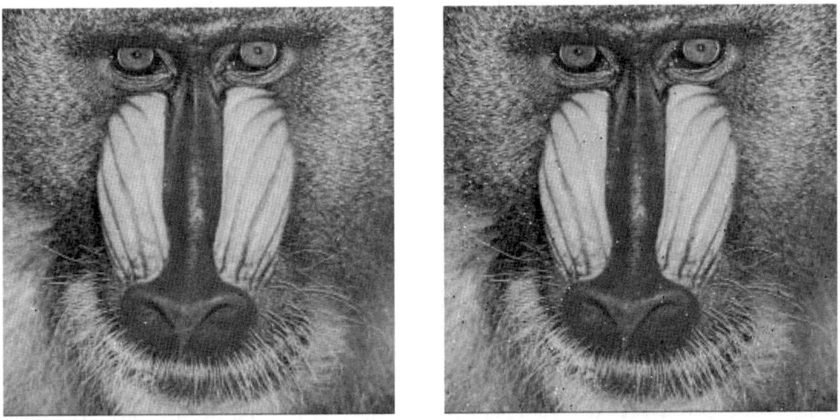

(a) (b)

Fig. 7. Two colluded *Baboon* images with (a) slow and (b) fast time-varying collusion attacks

time of a time-varying collusion attack with the channel coherent time in a communication system, which is a measure of the time duration over which the channel response is stationary [44, 45, 46, 28] so that the coefficients are nearly constant.

To give an example, we embed fingerprints into the Baboon image of size 256×256. We scan the image from top-left to bottom-right in the row-wise fashion so that a time index can be associated with pixels. Figs. 7 (a) and (b) show two attacked images with slow and fast time-varying collusion attacks by 200 colluders. There exists no noticeable difference between the original image and the colluded image in Fig. 7 (a). In contrast, the colluded image with fast time-varying attack contains visible artifacts which appear in form of salt and pepper noise.

5 Open Research Problems

There are several open problems to be addressed in the future.

- Design of robust fingerprinting systems
  To design a fingerprinting system against time-varying collusion attacks is the goal of the MC-CDMA-based fingerprinting system. However, how to tackle fast time-varying collusion attacks effectively remains a challenge.
- Analysis of flexible fingerprinting systems
  It is worthwhile to conduct quantitative analysis on the relationship of the quality of colluded media files, the attack rate and the number of colluders. It is also interesting to characterize the colluder detection performance as a function of the attack rate and the number of colluders. The goal is to get a sufficiently high colluder detection rate when the quality of the colluded file is acceptable.

– Time-varying collusion attacks
The relationship between the changing rate of time-varying colluder weights and media distortions is still not well understood. With a better understanding on this relationship, it might be possible to design fast time-varying collusion attacks without distortion from attacker's viewpoint and it would demand more research in their countermeasures from the defender's viewpoint.

6 Conclusion

In this work, we examined the time-varying collusion attack problem and solved it using an analogy drawn from wireless communications. We provided a review on the MC-CDMA-based fingerprinting system as well as preliminary results on capacity analysis based on the HVS model, throughput analysis on the number of allowed colluders, quality degradation of colluded media due to the attack rate and the number of colluders. Finally, we presented open research problems in this dynamic and challenging field.

References

1. Stone, H.S.: Analysis of attacks on image watermarks with randomized coefficients. Technical Report 96-045, NEC Res. Inst. Tech. Princeton, NJ (1996)
2. Yacobi, Y.: Improved Boneh-Shaw content fingerprinting. In: Naccache, D. (ed.) CT-RSA 2001. LNCS, vol. 2020, p. 378. Springer, Heidelberg (2001)
3. Liu, K.J.R., Trappe, W., Wang, Z.J., Wu, M., Zhao, H.: Multimedia fingerprinting forensics for traitor tracing. In: Hindawi, EURASIP on Signal Processing and Communications, New York, NY (2005)
4. Blackley, G.R., Meadows, C., Purdy, G.B.: Fingerprinting long forgiving messages. In: Proc. of Cryptography, Berlin, Heidelberg, pp. 180–189 (1985)
5. Cha, B.H., Kuo, C.C.J.: Design of collusion-free codes based on MAI-free principle. In: Proc. IEEE Int'l. Conf. Intelligent Information Hiding and Multimedia Signal Processing, Pasadena, CA, December 2006, pp. 639–642 (2006)
6. Cha, B.H., Kuo, C.C.J.: Design of collusion-free hiding codes using MAI-free principle. In: Proc. IEEE Int'l. Conf. Acoustics, Speech, and Signal Processing, Honolulu, HI, April 2007, pp. 145–148 (2007)
7. Cha, B.H., Kuo, C.C.J.: Design of multiuser collusion-free hiding codes with delayed embedding. In: Proc. IEEE Int'l. Conf. Intelligent Information Hiding and Multimedia Signal Processing, Kaohsiung, Taiwan, November 2007, pp. 379–382 (2007)
8. Cha, B.H., Kuo, C.C.J.: Design and analysis of high-capacity anti-collusion hiding codes. Journal of Circuits, Systems, and Signal Processing 27, 195–211 (2008)
9. Cha, B.H., Kuo, C.C.J.: Advanced colluder detection techniques for OSIFT-based hiding codes. In: Proc. IEEE Int'l. Sym. Circuits and Systems, Seattle, Washington, May 2008, pp. 2961–2964 (2008)
10. Cha, B.H., Kuo, C.C.J.: Analysis of time-varying collusion attacks in fingerprinting systems: capacity and throughput. In: Proc. IEEE Int'l. Sym. Circuits and Systems, Taipei, Taiwan, May 2009, pp. 493–496 (2009)

11. Cha, B.H., Kuo, C.C.J.: Robust MC-CDMA-based fingerprinting against time-varying collusion attacks. IEEE Transactions on Information Forensics and Security 4, 302–317 (2009)
12. Kiyavash, N., Moulin, P.: A framework for optimizing nonlinear collusion attack on fingerprinting systems. In: Proc. Conf. Infromation Sciences and Systems, Princeton, NJ (2006)
13. Kiyavash, N., Moulin, P.: On optimal collusion strategies for fingerprinting. In: Proc. IEEE Int'l. Conf. Acoustics, Speech, and Signal Processing, Toulouse, France, May 2006, pp. 405–408 (2006)
14. Zhao, H.V., Liu, K.J.R.: Tritor-within-traitor behavior forensics: strategy and risk minimization. IEEE Transactions on Information Forensics and Security 1, 440–456 (2006)
15. Zhao, H.V., Wu, M., Wang, Z.J., Liu, K.J.R.: Forensic analysis of nonlinear collusion attacks for multimedia fingerpinting. IEEE Transactions on Image Processing 14, 646–661 (2005)
16. Wang, Z.J., Wu, M., Zhao, H.V., Liu, K.J.R.: Anti-collusion forensics of multimedia fingerprinting using orthogonal mudulation. IEEE Transactions on Image Processing 14, 804–821 (2005)
17. Staddon, J.N., Stinson, D.R., Wei, R.: Combinatorial properties of frameproof and traceability codes. IEEE Transactions on Information Theory 47, 1042–1049 (2001)
18. Wagner, N.R.: Fingerprinting. In: Proc. Symp. Security Privacy, Oakland, CA, April 1983, pp. 18–22 (1983)
19. Hollmann, H.D.L., van Lint, J.H., Linnartz, J.P., Tolhuizen, L.M.G.M.: On codes with the identifiable parent property. Journal of Combinatorial Theory 82, 121–133 (1998)
20. Boneh, D., Shaw, J.: Collusion-secure fingerprinting for digital data. IEEE Transactions on Information Theory 44, 1897–1905 (1998)
21. Chor, B., Fiat, A., Naor, M., Pinkas, B.: Tracing traitors. IEEE Transactions on Information Theory 46, 893–910 (2000)
22. Tardos, G.: Optimal probabilistic fingerprint coding. In: Proc. ACM symp. Theory Comput., pp. 116–125 (2003)
23. Wu, M., Trappe, W., Wang, Z.J., Liu, K.J.R.: Collusion resistant fingerprinting for multimedia. IEEE Signal Processing Magazine 21, 15–27 (2004)
24. Cox, I.J., Kilian, J., Leighton, F.T., Shamoon, T.: Secure spread spectrum watermarking for multimedia. IEEE Transactions on Image Processing 6, 1673–1687 (1997)
25. Li, Z., Trappe, W.: Collusion-resistant fingerprints from WBE sequence sets. In: Proc. IEEE Int'l. Conf. Communications, Seoul, Korea, May 2005, pp. 1336–1340 (2005)
26. Trappe, W., Wu, M., Wang, Z.J., Liu, K.J.R.: Anti-collusion fingerprinting for multimedia. IEEE Transactions on Signal Processing 51, 1069–1087 (2003)
27. He, S., Wu, M.: Joint coding and embedding techniques for multimedia fingerprinting. IEEE Transactions on Information Forensics and Security 1, 231–247 (2006)
28. Tse, D.N.C., Viswanath, P.: Fundamentals of wireless communication. Cambridge University Press, Cambridge (2005)
29. Tsai, S.H., Lin, Y.P., Kuo, C.C.J.: A precoded multiuser OFDM (PMU-OFDM) transceiver for time asynchronous systems. In: Proc. IEEE GLOBECOM, St. Louis, MO, November 2005, pp. 2214–2218 (2005)
30. Tsai, S.H., Lin, Y.P., Kuo, C.C.J.: MAI-free MC-CDMA based on Hadamard-Walsh codes. IEEE Transactions on Signal Processing 54, 3166–3179 (2006)

31. Giannakis, G.B., Serpedin, E.: Linear multichannel blind equalizers of nonlinear FIR volterra channels. IEEE Transactions on Signal Processing 45, 67–81 (1997)
32. Tugnait, J.K., Tong, L., Ding, Z.: Single-user channel estimation and equalization. IEEE Signal Processing Magazine 17, 16–28 (2000)
33. Verdu, S.: Multiuser detection. Cambridge University Press, Cambridge (1998)
34. Hanzo, L., Munster, M., Choi, B.J., Keller, T.: OFDM and MC-CDMA for broadband multi-user communications, WLANs and broadcasting. John Wiley & Sons, West Sussex (2004)
35. Jayant, N., Johnston, J., Safranek, R.: Signal compression based on models of human perception. Proceedings of the IEEE 81, 1385–1422 (1993)
36. Watson, A.B.: DCT quantization matrices visually optimized for individual images. In: Proc. SPIE, Conf. Human Vision, Visual Processing, and Digital Display, San Jose, CA, USA, February 1993, pp. 202–216 (1993)
37. Watson, A.B., Yang, G.Y., Solomon, J.A., Villasenor, J.: Visibility of wavelet qunatization noise. IEEE Transactions on Image Processing 6, 1164–1175 (1997)
38. Podilchuk, C.I., Zeng, W.: Image-adaptive watermarking using visual models. IEEE Journal on Selected Areas in Communications 16, 525–539 (1998)
39. Kirovski, D., Malvar, H.S.: Spread-spectrum watermarking of audio signals. IEEE Transactions on Signal Processing 51, 1020–1033 (2003)
40. Liu, Y.W., Smith, J.O.: Audio watermarking through deterministic plus stochastic signal decomposition. EURASIP Journal on Information Security 2007, 1–12 (2007)
41. Allen, J.B., Rabiner, L.R.: A unified approach to short-time Fourier analaysis and synthesis. Proceedings of the IEEE 65, 1558–1564 (1977)
42. Princen, J.P., Bradley, A.B.: Analysis/synthesis filter bank design based on time domain aliasing cancellation. IEEE Transactions on Acoustics, Speech, and Signal Processing 86, 1153–1161 (1986)
43. Tse, D.N.C., Hanly, S.V.: Linear multiuser receivers: effective interference, effective bandwidth and user capacity. IEEE Transactions on Information Theory 45, 641–657 (1999)
44. Proakis, J.G.: Digital Communications. McGraw-Hill, New York (1995)
45. Sklar, B.: Rayleigh fading channels in mobile digital communications systems part I: characterization. IEEE Communications Magazine, 90–100 (July 1997)
46. Sklar, B.: Rayleigh fading channels in mobile digital communications systems part II: mitigation. IEEE Communications Magazine, 102–109 (July 1997)

Phase-Only Correlation Based Matching in Scrambled Domain for Preventing Illegal Matching

Izumi Ito and Hitoshi Kiya

Graduate School of System Design, Tokyo Metropolitan University
6-6 Asahigaoka, Hino-shi, Tokyo, Japan
kiya@sd.tmu.ac.jp

Abstract. We herein propose an image matching in the scrambled domain for preventing illegal image matching, which is defined as a malicious and intentional act conducted in order to deduce the content of images. The phase of discrete Fourier transform (DFT) coefficients of images is scrambled for visual protection. In addition, the magnitude of DFT coefficients is scrambled for preventing illegal image matching. Phase-only correlation (POC) or phase correlation can be applied directly to images in the scrambled domain for alignment and similarity. The accuracy of POC in the scrambled domain is the same as that in the non-scrambled domain. Simulations are presented to confirm the appropriateness and effectiveness of the proposed scrambling.

Keywords: phase-only correlation, image matching, visual protection, illegal image matching.

1 Introduction

Phase-only correlation or phase correlation, which is referred to as POC in the present paper, is used to estimate the similarity and translation between two signals. POC in terms with Fourier transform was developed as PHAse Transform in [1] and POC in terms with discrete Fourier transform (DFT) was proposed by Kuglin and Hines in [2]. The concept of the POC is based on the Fourier shift property, and the estimation of translation is extended to the estimation of rotated and scaled values between two images by log-polar coordinate change [3]. A number of subpixel estimation methods have been proposed [4]-[8], and high-accuracy techniques for POC have been developed [9]. The estimation of geometrically converted values enables POC to be an effective method for image matching [10]-[13]. In POC-based image matching, images are stored in the form of images or their DFT coefficients as templates in a database. As a result, if templates were leaked, unlike templates that consist of statistical feature of images, the contents of the templates are revealed. Generally, encrypting is used for protection [14]-[16]. However, encrypted images require decrypting before image matching. In addition, decrypting of a multitude of templates requires enormous

Y.Q. Shi (Ed.): Transactions on DHMS V, LNCS 6010, pp. 51–69, 2010.

computational complexity, and after image matching, decrypted images have to be discarded so as not to cause a security problem. Therefore, signal processing in an encrypted domain is desired [17] [18].

Based on this background, we previously proposed phase scrambling that protects the information of the original image visually [19] [20] for POC and DCT sign phase correlation [21]. However, since phase scrambling protects only the phase information, the phase scrambling does not prevent the templates from being deduced by the magnitude of DFT coefficients (DFT magnitude) of the templates.

In the present paper, we propose a matching system in which both the phase information and the magnitude of DFT coefficients of templates are protected. First, direct DFT magnitude scrambling is considered in order to show the problem of scrambling of the DFT magnitude. Next, based on the processes of image matching, we propose a scrambling method for the DFT magnitude, in which the phase information of the log-polar transformed DFT magnitude is scrambled. In typical image matching system using POC, after alignment for rotation and scaling, the matching score is calculated. In the proposed scrambling method, not only rotated and scaled values for alignment are estimated by POC without descrambling but also the matching score can be calculated by POC without descrambling. Moreover, the values estimated by POC between signals which are scrambled with the same key are mathematically ensured to be the same as those estimated by POC between non-scrambled signals. Also, since the proposed scrambling disperse the correlation peak in the case of different key, the proposed scrambling has the effectiveness of preventing illegal image matching, which is the malicious and intentional deduction of the content of the template by POC. The experimental results of preventing illegal image matching show the effectiveness and appropriateness of the proposed method.

2 Preliminary

In this section, phase-only correlation and phase scrambling are explained. Single-dimensional notation is used for the sake of brevity. Integer values, n, n_1, and n_2 denote the indices of signals in the space domain, and integer values, k, k_1, and k_2 denote the indices of signals in the frequency domain.

2.1 Goal of the Present Study

In an image matching system composed of a multitude of templates, template security is an important consideration. Specifically, the matching system using POC requires templates to be hidden from view, because the POC requires the templates to be either original images or phase information of original images.

Figure 1 illustrates the relationship between the strongly protected area and matching systems using POC. Figure 1(a) shows a typical matching system using POC, in which the templates are visible, and a broad area that includes the database should be strongly protected. If the templates were leaked, the original image will be revealed. Figure 1(b) shows an encrypted template matching

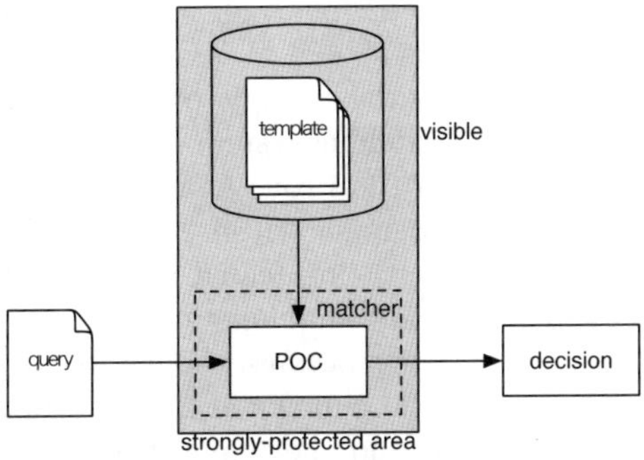

(a) typical matching system using POC.

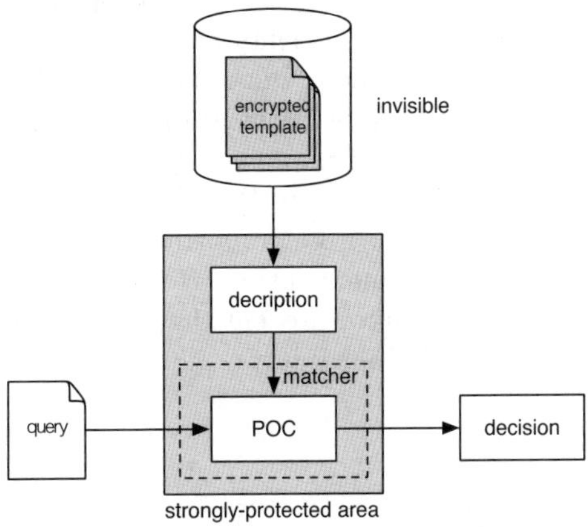

(b) encrypted template matching system using POC.

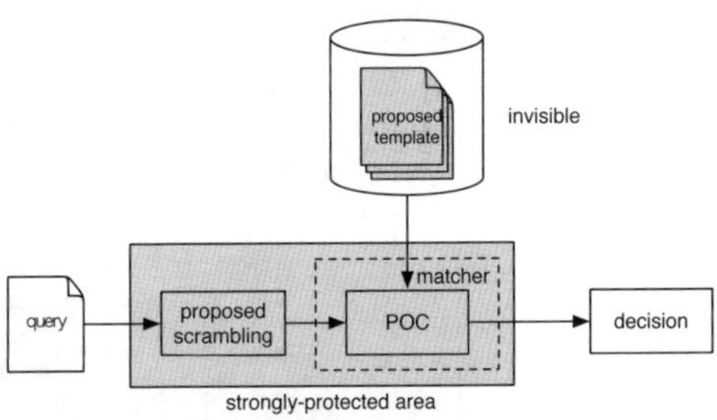

(c) proposed matching system using POC.

Fig. 1. Relationship between strongly protected area and matching systems using POC. (a) Typical matching system, in which the templates are visible and result in compromise. A broad area that includes the database should be strongly protected. (b) Encrypted template matching system, in which the templates are encrypted and invisible. However, the decryption of each template is required in the matching process. (c) Proposed matching system, in which the templates are scrambled and invisible. Instead of descrambling of each template, the proposed scrambling is required for a query in the matching process. The strongly protected area can be narrowed as suitably as the encrypted template matching system.

system using POC, in which each template for a query is decrypted, and after image matching, decrypted images should be removed, although the templates are invisible due to encryption and the strongly protected area can be narrowed. Figure 1(c) shows the proposed matching system using POC, in which templates are invisible and which can narrow the strongly protected area as suitably as the encrypted template matching system shown in Fig. 1(b). In addition, the proposed matching system can handle the protected templates directly. As a result, compared to the encrypted template matching system, the proposed matching system has high processing efficiency, because the number of the scrambling operations for a query is less than the number of the decrypting operations for a multitude of templates generally, and the removal of decrypted images is not required.

Figure 2 illustrates phase scrambling, which we proposed previously [19] [20], for visual protection. The DFT coefficients of an image are composed of the phase information and the magnitude. Once the inverse DFT is applied to either the DFT coefficients or the phase information, the information of the image is exposed, while the inverse DFT of the magnitude of DFT coefficients is invisible and does not expose the information. Based on these considerations, phase scrambling protects the templates from important information being revealed visually by distorting the phase information. However, since the DFT magnitude is untouched, the system cannot prevent the information of templates from being deduced based on the DFT magnitude.

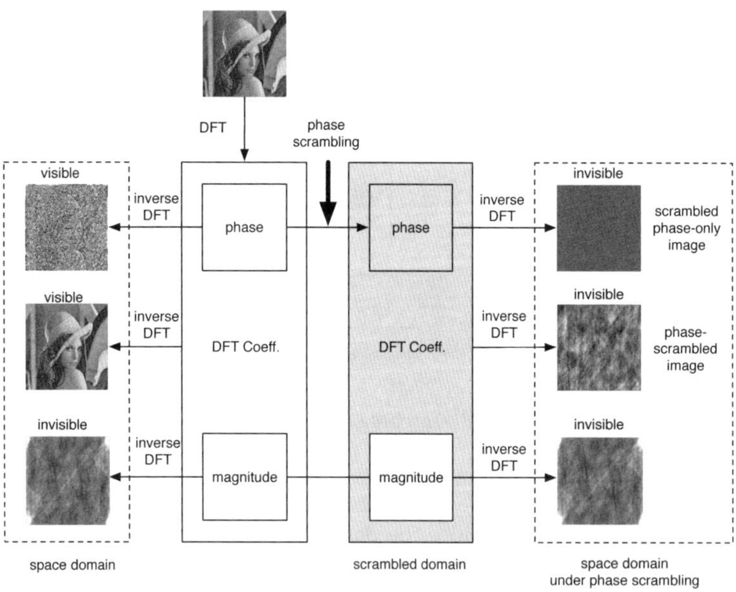

Fig. 2. Phase scrambling for visual protection. Phase scrambling protects the visual content of the original image.

In the present paper, we consider the scrambling of the DFT magnitude and an image matching system in which templates are invisible and POC can be applied without descrambling. We assume that the other levels of attacks are strongly protected, except for the case in which leakage of templates occurs.

2.2 Phase-Only Correlation (POC)

Translation. Let $G_i(k)$ be the N-point DFT coefficients of the N-point signal $g_i(n)$ which are real numbers. The phase term, $\phi_{G_i}(k)$, is defined as

$$\phi_{G_i}(k) = G_i(k)/|G_i(k)| = e^{j\theta_i(k)} \tag{1}$$

where $|G_i(k)|$ denotes the magnitude of $G_i(k) = |G_i(k)|e^{j\theta_i(k)}$, j denotes $\sqrt{-1}$, and if $|G_i(k)| = 0$, then $\phi_{G_i}(k) = e^{j\theta_i(k)}$ is replaced by zero.

Let $G_1(k)$ and $G_2(k)$ be N-point DFT coefficients of the N-point signals $g_1(n)$ and $g_2(n)$ which are real numbers, respectively. The normalized cross spectrum, $R_\phi(k)$, is defined as

$$R_\phi(k) = \phi^*_{G_1}(k) \cdot \phi_{G_2}(k) \tag{2}$$

where $\phi^*_{G_1}(k)$ denotes the complex conjugate of $\phi_{G_1}(k)$. The POC is defined by the inverse DFT of $R_\phi(k)$ as

$$r_\phi(n) = \frac{1}{N}\sum_{k=0}^{N-1} R_\phi(k) W_N^{-nk} \tag{3}$$

where W_N denotes $\exp(-j2\pi/N)$. The translation between $g_1(n)$ and $g_2(n)$ are estimated by the location n of the maximum correlation value $\gamma =^{\max}_{n} (r_\phi(n))$ [2].

Rotation and scaling. In the estimation of rotated and scaled values, the magnitude of DFT coefficients (DFT magnitude) is regarded as an image in the space domain, and the coordinates of the DFT magnitude are mapped in log-polar order so that the rotated and scaled values reduce to the horizontal and vertical translations, respectively.

Let $|G_i(k_1, k_2)|$ be the $N \times N$-point DFT magnitude of the $N \times N$-point image $g_i(n_1, n_2)$. The DFT magnitude $|G_i(k_1, k_2)|$ is altered into a new image, $g_{i_{LP}}(n_1, n_2)$, consisting of the same intensity values, but arranged in new positions:

$$g_{i_{LP}}(n_1, n_2) = \mathrm{LP}\left[|G_i(k_1, k_2)|\right] \tag{4}$$

where LP denotes log-polar mapping. In the present paper, $g_{i_{LP}}(n_1, n_2)$ is referred to as the log-polar image. In practice, the intensity of the DFT magnitude is interpolated in order to convert a digital image into an analog image in the process of log-polar mapping.

Let $g_{1_{LP}}(n_1, n_2)$ and $g_{2_{LP}}(n_1, n_2)$ be log-polar images of $g_1(n_1, n_2)$ and $g_2(n_1, n_2)$, respectively. In addition, let $G_{1_{LP}}(k_1, k_2)$ and $G_{2_{LP}}(k_1, k_2)$ be the DFT coefficients of $g_{1_{LP}}(n_1, n_2)$ and $g_{2_{LP}}(n_1, n_2)$, respectively. The rotated and scaled values are estimated from the location of the maximum correlation value, γ_{LP}, of the POC, $r_{\phi_{LP}}(n_1, n_2)$, between $g_{1_{LP}}(n_1, n_2)$ and $g_{2_{LP}}(n_1, n_2)$, that is,

$$r_{\phi_{LP}}(n_1, n_2) = \frac{1}{N^2} \sum_{k_1=0}^{N-1} \sum_{k_2=0}^{N-1} R_{\phi_{LP}}(k_1, k_2) W_N^{-n_1 k_1} W_N^{-n_2 k_2} \tag{5}$$

where

$$R_{\phi_{LP}}(k_1, k_2) = \phi^*_{G_{1_{LP}}}(k_1, k_2) \cdot \phi_{G_{2_{LP}}}(k_1, k_2) \ . \tag{6}$$

The locations n_1 and n_2 of $\gamma_{LP} =^{\max}_{n_1, n_2} r_{\phi_{LP}}(n_1, n_2)$ correspond to the rotated and scaled values between $g_1(n_1, n_2)$ and $g_2(n_1, n_2)$, respectively [3].

2.3 Phase Scrambling

Visual protection. Phase scrambling is accomplished by multiplying N-point DFT coefficients of an N-point signal by the phase term of an N-point key sequence, $\theta_{\alpha_i}(k)$, i.e.,

$$\widetilde{G}_i(k) = G_i(k) \cdot e^{j\theta_{\alpha_i}(k)} \ . \tag{7}$$

Replacing $G_i(k)$ in Eq. (7) by its polar form yields

$$\widetilde{G}_i(k) = |G_i(k)| \phi_{G_i}(k) \cdot e^{j\theta_{\alpha_i}(k)} \ . \tag{8}$$

Therefore, phase scrambling affects only the phase of DFT coefficients,

$$\widetilde{\phi}_{G_i}(k) = \phi_{G_i}(k) \cdot e^{j\theta_{\alpha_i}(k)} \ . \tag{9}$$

The phase scrambling in Eq. (9) protects the visual information of the original image. In [19] [20], the element of a key sequence is either 0 or π, which corresponds to $\exp(j0) = 1$ or $\exp(j\pi) = -1$, respectively.

Image matching in the scrambled domain. From Eqs. (2) and (9), the normalized cross spectrum, $\widetilde{R}_\phi(k)$, under phase scrambling is given as

$$\begin{aligned} \widetilde{R}_\phi(k) &= \phi^*_{G_1}(k) \cdot \phi_{G_2}(k) \\ &= \phi^*_{G_1}(k) e^{-j\theta_{\alpha_1}(k)} \cdot \phi_{G_2}(k) e^{j\theta_{\alpha_2}(k)} \ . \end{aligned} \tag{10}$$

If $\theta_{\alpha_1}(k) = \theta_{\alpha_2}(k)$, then

$$e^{-j\theta_{\alpha_1}(k)} \cdot e^{j\theta_{\alpha_2}(k)} = 1 \ . \tag{11}$$

Therefore, from Eqs. (2), (10), and (11), we obtain

$$\widetilde{R}_\phi(k) = R_\phi(k) \ . \tag{12}$$

There is no effect of scrambling on the normalized cross spectrum in the case of the same key sequences. That is, mathematically, the translation and the maximum correlation value estimated by the POC between non-scrambled signals can be obtained from the POC between two signals which are scrambled with the same key sequences.

2.4 A Key Sequence and Its Update

A key sequence. The length of a key sequence is required the length of a signal, i.e., N-point key sequence is required for scrambling of an N-point signal. The N-point key sequence, $\theta_{\alpha_i}(k)$, $k = 0, 1, \cdots, N-1$, is determined from a set $U_{x_1}^M$ that consists of M-member, x_1,x_2,$\cdots$,x_M, $(M \leq N)$, i.e.,

$$\theta_{\alpha_i}(k) \in U_{x_1}^M, \quad U_{x_1}^M = \{x_1, x_2, \cdots, x_M\} \ . \tag{13}$$

In two-dimensional expression, $N \times N$-point key sequence, $\theta_{\alpha_i}(k_1, k_2)$, $k_1 = 0, 1, \cdots, N-1$, $k_2 = 0, 1, \cdots, N-1$ is required for scrambling an $N \times N$-point signal. In [19] [20], the element of a key sequence is in $U_0^2 = \{0, \pi\}$, which corresponds to $\exp(j0) = 1$ or $\exp(j\pi) = -1$. Generally, the element of a key sequence can be set using random numbers with a key, α_i. In the case of using random numbers, phase scrambling is analogous to a stream cipher [22]. The key space of the key sequence is determined from the size of image, $N \times N$, the number of members, M, and how to generate random numbers. If true random numbers are generated, the key space is $M^{N \times N}$.

The effectiveness of preventing illegal image matching is considered in terms of probability. A large number of the cases in which the value of an element of a key sequence is different from the value of the corresponding element of another key sequence increases the effectiveness of preventing illegal image matching. Let two key sequences be $\theta_{\alpha_1}(k)$ and $\theta_{\alpha_2}(k)$, where $\theta_{\alpha_i}(k) \in U_{x_1}^2$ and $U_{x_1}^2 = \{x_1, x_2\}$. Let q_{x_1} be the occurrence probability of x_1 per element. The probability, $Q_2(q_{x_1}, q_{x_2})$, that satisfies $\theta_{\alpha_1}(k) = \theta_{\alpha_2}(k)$ for any k is given as

$$Q_2(q_{x_1}, q_{x_2})|_{q_{x_1}=1-q_{x_2}} = q_{x_1}^2 + (1-q_{x_1})^2 = 2\left(q_a - \frac{1}{2}\right)^2 + \frac{1}{2} \ . \tag{14}$$

Therefore, $Q_2(q_{x_1}, q_{x_2})$ gives the minimum value of 1/2 when $q_{x_1} = 0.5$. The effectiveness of preventing illegal image matching with $q_{x_1} = 0.5$ will be shown in Section 4.

Next, a set with M-member $U_{x_1}^M$ is considered. We assume that each occurrence probability q_{x_i}, $i = 1, 2, \cdots, M$ is the same. The probability, $Q_M(q_{x_1}, q_{x_2}, \cdots, q_{x_M})$, that satisfies $\theta_{\alpha_1}(k) = \theta_{\alpha_2}(k)$ for any k is given as

$$Q_M(q_{x_1}, q_{x_2}, \cdots, q_{x_M})\big|_{q_{x_1}=q_{x_2}=\cdots=q_{x_M}} = M\frac{1}{M^2} = \frac{1}{M} \ . \tag{15}$$

A large number of members in a set enhances the effectiveness of preventing illegal image matching with respect to coincident probability [23].

Update of a key sequence. The key sequence is renewable. At regular intervals or when the database has been accessed illegally, the key sequence can be renewed, and the templates can be updated without descrambling. The updated key sequence $\theta'_{\alpha_i}(k)$ is given by the addition of new key sequence $\eta_{\alpha_i}(k)$ as

$$\theta'_{\alpha_i}(k) = \theta_{\alpha_i}(k) + \eta_{\alpha_i}(k) \ . \tag{16}$$

For instance, the phase term protected by scrambling with key sequence $\theta_{\alpha_i}(k)$ can be updated directly by multiplying $\widetilde{\phi}_i(k) = \phi_i(k)e^{j\theta_{\alpha_i}(k)}$ by $\exp(j\eta_{\alpha_i}(k))$:

$$\begin{aligned}\widetilde{\phi}'_i(k) &= \phi_i(k)e^{j\theta_{\alpha_i}(k)} \cdot e^{j\eta_{\alpha_i}(k)} \\ &= \phi_i(k)e^{j\theta'_{\alpha_i}(k)} \ . \end{aligned} \tag{17}$$

The updated key sequence, $\theta'_{\alpha_i}(k)$, is used for a query in the matching process after updating the templates.

3 Scrambling for the DFT Magnitude

We propose a scrambling method for the DFT magnitude, in which the phase information of log-polar image is scrambled, in order to prevent illegal image matching.

3.1 Direct DFT Magnitude Scrambling

In order to clarify the problem of scrambling of the DFT magnitude, direct DFT magnitude scrambling is introduced. Direct DFT magnitude scrambling is based on an analogy of phase scrambling. Direct DFT magnitude scrambling is accomplished by multiplying the $N \times N$-point key sequence $r_{\beta_i}(k_1, k_2)$ by the DFT magnitude, where $r_{\beta_i}(k_1, k_2) \in \mathbb{R}$ and $\mathbb{R}$ denotes a set of real numbers.

In direct DFT magnitude scrambling, the scrambled DFT magnitude, $\widetilde{G}_i(k_1, k_2)$, is given as

$$\widetilde{G}_i(k_1, k_2) = |G_i(k_1, k_2)| \cdot r_{\beta_i}(k_1, k_2) \ . \tag{18}$$

From Eq. (4), the scrambled log-polar image $\widetilde{g}_{i_{LP}}(n_1, n_2)$ is given as

$$\widetilde{g}_{i_{LP}}(n_1, n_2) = \mathrm{LP}\left[|G_i(k_1, k_2)|\, r_{\beta_i}(k_1, k_2)\right] \ . \tag{19}$$

If $r_{\beta_i}(k_1, k_2)$ is a constant, C_i, for all k_1 and k_2, then $\widetilde{g}_{i_{LP}}(n_1, n_2)$ is expressed as

$$\widetilde{g}_{i_{LP}}(n_1, n_2) = C_i g_{i_{LP}}(n_1, n_2) \ . \tag{20}$$

In this case, the normalized cross spectrum $\widetilde{R}_{\phi_{LP}}(k_1, k_2)$ between $\widetilde{g}_{1_{LP}}(n_1, n_2)$ and $\widetilde{g}_{2_{LP}}(n_1, n_2)$ is equal to $R_{\phi_{LP}}(k_1, k_2)$. In other words, illegal image matching is not prevented. Moreover, if $r_{\beta_i}(k_1, k_2)$ is not a constant, then $\widetilde{g}_{i_{LP}}(n_1, n_2)$ cannot be expressed by the non-scrambled log-polar image, $g_{i_{LP}}(n_1, n_2)$, because of the practical limitation that occurs as a result of the interpolation applied during transformation into log-polar coordinates. Even if interpolation does not affect the log-polar mapping, the scrambling of a log-polar image cannot be canceled by the scrambling with the same key sequence. Namely, the rotation angle and scale factor cannot be estimated correctly by POC under scrambling. Therefore, direct DFT magnitude scrambling is not useful in achieving our goal.

3.2 Phase Scrambling of Log-Polar Image

We propose a scrambling method for the DFT magnitude, which involves scrambling the phase information of a log-polar image that is converted from the DFT magnitude. Theoretically, the proposed method not only ensures the same values estimated by POC between non-scrambled images but also reduces the computational load for descrambling of templates in a system.

Let $G_{i_{LP}}(k_1, k_2)$ be the $N \times N$-point DFT coefficients of $N \times N$-point log-polar image $g_{i_{LP}}(n_1, n_2)$. The scrambled DFT coefficients, $\widetilde{G}_{i_{LP}}(k_1, k_2)$, are obtained by multiplying $G_{i_{LP}}(k_1, k_2)$ by the phase term of an $N \times N$-point key sequence $\theta_{\beta_i}(k_1, k_2)$:

$$\widetilde{G}_{i_{LP}}(k_1, k_2) = G_{i_{LP}}(k_1, k_2) \cdot e^{j\theta_{\beta_i}(k_1,k_2)} \ . \tag{21}$$

The normalized cross spectrum $\widetilde{R}_{\phi_{LP}}(k_1, k_2)$ between $\widetilde{G}_{1_{LP}}(k_1, k_2)$ and $\widetilde{G}_{2_{LP}}(k_1, k_2)$ is given as

$$\widetilde{R}_{\phi_{LP}}(k_1, k_2) = \phi^*_{G_{1_{LP}}}(k_1, k_2) e^{-j\theta_{\beta_1}(k_1,k_2)} \cdot \phi_{G_{2_{LP}}}(k_1, k_2) e^{j\theta_{\beta_2}(k_1,k_2)} \ . \tag{22}$$

If $\theta_{\beta_1}(k_1, k_2) = \theta_{\beta_2}(k_1, k_2)$, then

$$\widetilde{R}_{\phi_{LP}}(k_1, k_2) = R_{\phi_{LP}}(k_1, k_2) \ . \tag{23}$$

As long as the same interpolation method is used, the relative rotated and scaled values are preserved. In addition, the proposed method protects templates from illegal image matching.

The proposed scrambling is to scramble both phase information and DFT magnitude of an image. Figure 3 summarizes the steps of the proposed scrambling.

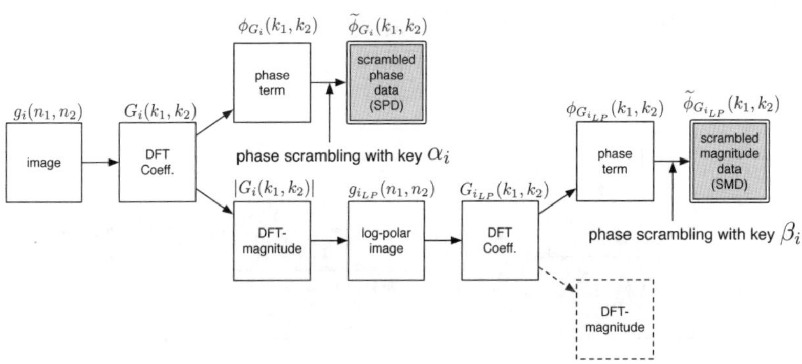

Fig. 3. Proposed scrambling. The DFT coefficients of an image are separated into the phase term and the DFT-magnitude. The phase term is directly phase-scrambled to obtain the scrambled phase data (SPD) with a key, α_i, while the DFT magnitude is transformed into a log-polar image, and the phase term of the log-polar image is phase-scrambled to obtain the scrambled magnitude data (SMD) with a key, β_i. The SPD and SMD can be used for POC.

3.3 System Model

Figure 4 shows a model of a system. The system has two main processes, namely, the template generation process and the image matching process. The steps of these two main processes are explained below.

Template generation process. Images are stored as templates in a database through the proposed scrambling. All templates registered in the database are scrambled by independent key sequences. Note that an independent key may be managed by individual.

The steps are as follows:

1. The DFT is applied to an image to obtain the DFT coefficients.
2. The phase term of the DFT coefficients is phase-scrambled with a key, α_i, to obtain the scrambled phase data (SPD).
3. The DFT magnitude, as shown in Fig. 5(b), is converted into a log-polar image (see Fig. 5(c)).
4. The DFT is applied to the log-polar image to obtain the DFT coefficients.

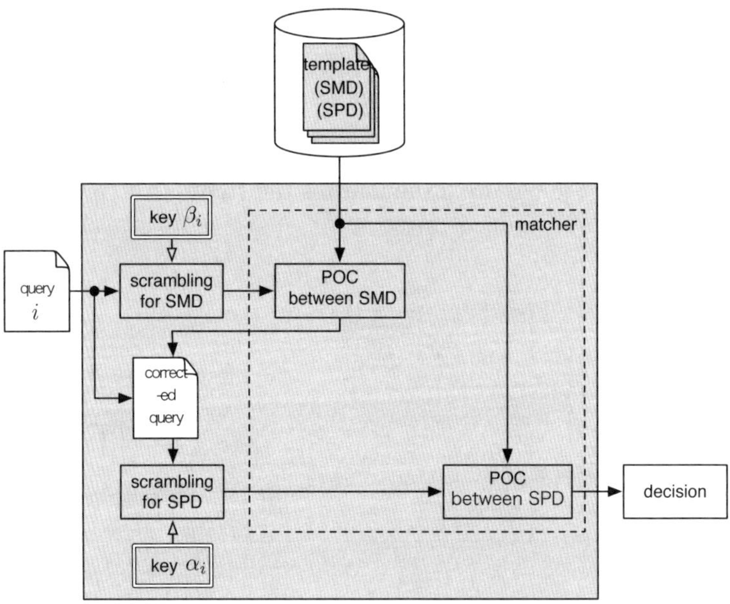

Fig. 4. System model (correction of rotation and scaling is required). When the database is queried, the scrambling for SMD is applied to a query, and POC between the SMD of the query and that of a template is calculated for correction of rotation and scaling of the query. After the corrected query is scrambled to obtain the SPD, the POC between the SPD of the corrected query and that of the template is calculated to obtain the matching score.

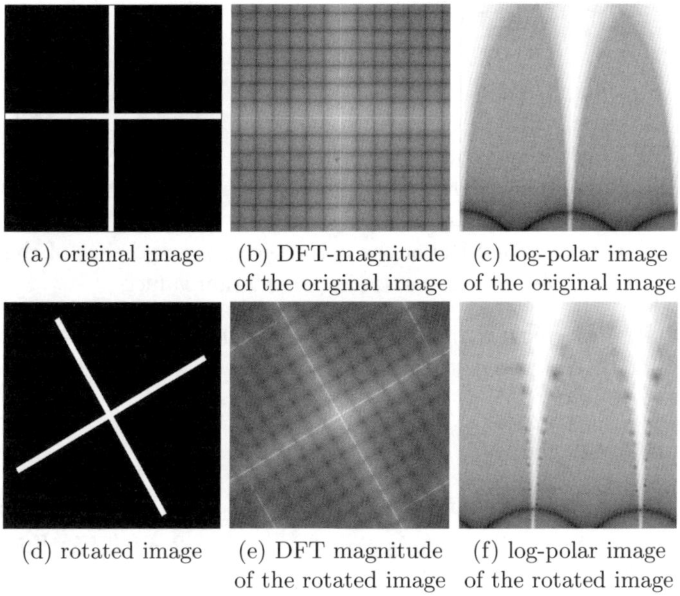

Fig. 5. Rotated image and log-polar image. (a) 512 × 512 monochrome image. (b) DFT magnitude of (a). (c) Log-polar image of (b). (d) Rotated image of (a). (e) DFT magnitude of (d). (f) Log-polar image of (e).

5. The phase term of the DFT coefficients of the log-polar image is phase-scrambled with a key, β_i, to obtain the scrambled magnitude data (SMD).
6. The SPD and SMD are stored as a template.

Image matching process. The image matching process consists of alignment steps and matching steps. The alignment steps are performed in order to align a query or to call a template for matching steps in the database. The matching steps are performed in order to obtain the maximum correlation value used as a matching score.

Alignment steps

1. The DFT is applied to a query to obtain a DFT magnitude (see Fig. 5 (e)).
2. The DFT magnitude is transformed into a log-polar image (see Fig. 5 (f)).
3. The DFT is applied to the log-polar image to obtain the phase term of the DFT coefficients of the log-polar image.
4. The phase term is phase-scrambled with key β_i to obtain the SMD.
5. The POC between the SMD of the query and that of a template is calculated to estimate the rotated and scaled values.
6. The query is aligned by the estimated values to generate the corrected query.

In a typical matching system using POC, after alignment for rotation and scaling, the matching score is calculated. Therefore, among the alignment steps mentioned above, Step 4 is the only additional step for the proposed scrambling.

Matching steps

1. The DFT is applied to the corrected query to obtain the DFT coefficients.
2. The phase term of the DFT coefficients is scrambled with key α_i to obtain the SPD of the corrected query.
3. The POC between the SPD of the corrected query and that of the template is performed to obtain the maximum correlation value.

As compared to a typical matching system using POC, Step 2 is the only additional step for the proposed scrambling.

4 Simulation

In the following simulations, $N \times N$-point key sequences $\theta_{\alpha_i}(k_1, k_2)$ and $\theta_{\beta_i}(k_1, k_2)$ were determined from a two-member set $U^2_{\pi/2} = \{\pi/2, -\pi/2\}$ in Eq. (13). The occurence probability $x_{\pi/2}$ was 0.5.

4.1 Image Matching under the Proposed Scrambling

Image matching between two images, namely, a template and a query, was performed using POC. The query shown in Fig. 6(b) is generated from the template, which is the 256×256 8-bit monochrome image shown in Fig. 6(a), by translation, rotation and scaling, in which the rotation angle, φ, was five degrees and the scale factor, s, was 0.95. The POC between the template and the query was calculated in order to estimate the rotation angle and the scale factor. The estimated rotation angle, $\hat{\phi}$, and scale factor, $\hat{s}$, were 4.941 and 0.947, respectively. After correcting the query using $\hat{\phi}$ and $\hat{s}$, the POC between the template and the corrected query was calculated in order to obtain the maximum correlation value. The maximum correlation value, γ, was 0.495.

Next, the template was scrambled to obtain the SPD by Eq. (7) and SMD by Eq. (21) with the key sequences $\theta_{\alpha_1}(k_1, k_2)$ for SPD and $\theta_{\beta_1}(k_1, k_2)$ for SMD. Figure 6(c) shows the scrambled phase-only image of the template that is the inverse DFT of the SPD of the template. We can confirm that the original information of the template cannot be deduced by SPD. After the query was scrambled with the key sequence $\theta_{\beta_2}(k_1, k_2)$ to obtain the SMD, the POC between the SMD of the template and the SMD of the query was performed. Figures 7(a) and 7(b) show the POC surface between the SMDs with the same key sequences and the POC surface between the SMDs with different key sequences, respectively. In the case of using the same key sequences, i.e., $\theta_{\beta_1}(k_1, k_2) = \theta_{\beta_2}(k_1, k_2)$, the estimated rotation angle under scrambling, $\widetilde{\varphi}$, and the estimated scale factor under scrambling, $\widetilde{s}$, were 4.941 and 0.947, respectively, i.e., $\widetilde{\varphi} = \hat{\varphi}$ and $\widetilde{s} = \hat{s}$. We confirmed that the POC surface between the SMD of the template and the SMD of the query and the POC surface between non-scrambled images were

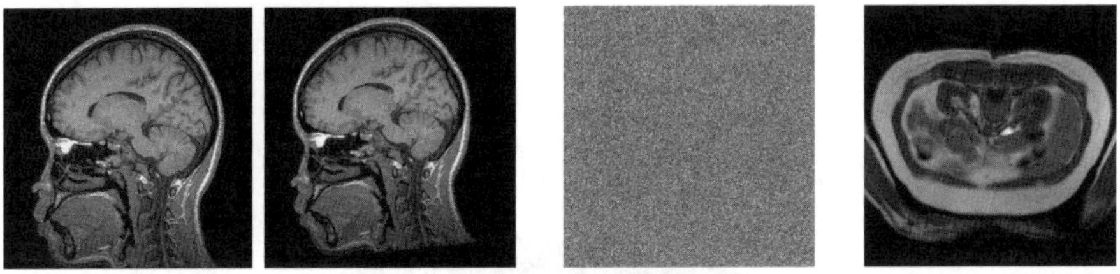

(a) template (b) query (head) (c) scrambled phase-only image of image (a) (d) query (liver)

Fig. 6. Test images. (a) 256 × 256 8-bit monochrome image. (b) Image generated from (a) by translation by five pixels in the horizontal and vertical directions, rotation by five degrees about the center of the image, and scaling by 0.95. (c) Scrambled phase-only image of (a). (d) 256 × 256 8-bit monochrome image.

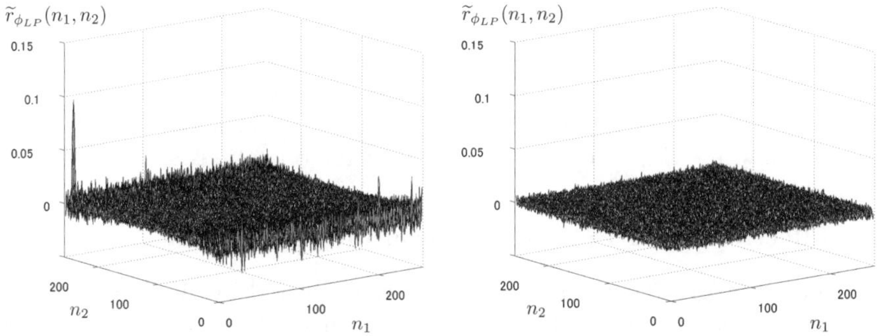

(a) with the same key sequences (b) with different key sequences.

Fig. 7. POC surface between the SMDs with the same key sequences and the SMDs with different key sequences. (a) When $\theta_{\beta_1}(k_1, k_2) = \theta_{\beta_2}(k_1, k_2)$, a distinct peak appears on the POC surface. (b) When $\theta_{\beta_1}(k_1, k_2) \neq \theta_{\beta_2}(k_1, k_2)$, no distinct peak appears on the POC surface.

identical as derived in Eq. (23). In the case of using different key sequences, i.e., $\theta_{\beta_1}(k_1, k_2) \neq \theta_{\beta_2}(k_1, k_2)$, $\widetilde{\varphi}$ and $\widetilde{s}$ were 32.4 and 3.03, respectively, i.e., $\widetilde{\varphi} \neq \hat{\varphi}$ and $\widetilde{s} \neq \hat{s}$. The rotation angle and scale factor could not be estimated correctly in the different key sequences. On the other hand, when only the phase information was scrambled, the POC surface under scrambling and the POC surface under non-scrambling were identical, although different key sequences were used.

After the query was corrected by $\widetilde{\varphi}$ and $\widetilde{s}$, the corrected query was scrambled with the key sequence, $\theta_{\alpha_2}(k_1, k_2)$, to obtain the SPD. The POC between the SPD of the template and the SPD of the corrected query was then performed. Figure 8 shows the POC surface between the SPDs with the same key sequences, in which the maximum correlation value under scrambling $\widetilde{\gamma}$ was 0.495, i.e., $\widetilde{\gamma} = \gamma$. The POC surface between the SPDs shown in Fig. 8 and the POC surface between non-scrambled images after correcting were identical. The proposed

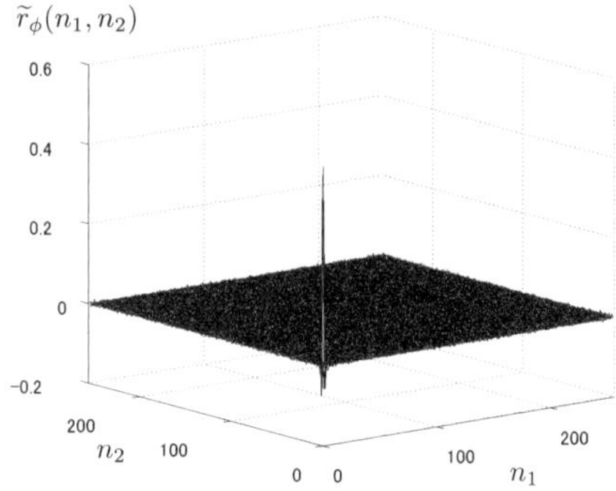

Fig. 8. POC surface between the SPDs with the same key sequences. A distinct peak appears on the POC surface. The POC surface between the SPDs and the POC surface between non-scrambled images after correcting were identical.

scrambling does not affect the values estimated by POC as derived in Eq. (12) mathematically, and has the effectiveness of preventing illegal image matching. The time for single scrambling was 18.7% of the time for single POC between two images, where the time was the average of 100 operations.

4.2 Effectiveness of Preventing Illegal Image Matching

The rotation angle and the scale factor were estimated by the POC between the SMD of the template and the SMD of the query. A total of 1000 different key sequences were used. The template shown in Fig. 6(a) was scrambled with $\theta_{\beta_0}(k_1, k_2)$ to obtain the SMD of the template. The query was rotated by φ degrees, scaled by s and scrambled with $\theta_{\beta_i}(k_1, k_2)$, $i = 1, 2, \cdots, 1000$ where $\theta_{\beta_0}(k_1, k_2) \neq \theta_{\beta_i}(k_1, k_2)$ to obtain the SMD of the query. $\widetilde{\varphi}$ and $\widetilde{s}$ are calculated from the location of the maximum correlation value under scrambling, $\widetilde{\gamma_{LP}}$.

Figure 9(a) shows 1000 sets of $\widetilde{\varphi}$ and $\widetilde{s}$ when Fig. 6(b) was used as the query where $\varphi = 5$ and $s = 0.95$, and Fig. 9(b) shows 1000 sets of $\widetilde{\varphi}$ and $\widetilde{s}$ when Fig. 6(d) was used as the query where $\varphi = 5$ degree and $s = 0.95$. The dispersion of 1000 sets shown in Fig. 9(a) in which the query was the same as the template was similar to the dispersion of 1000 sets shown in Fig. 9(b) in which the query was different from the template. Therefore, we can conclude that the proposed scrambling has the effect of preventing illegal image matching by POC in order to deduce the template. Figures 9(c) and 9(d) show the magnification of Figs 9(a) and 9(b), respectively. There was no point in which $\widetilde{\varphi} = \hat{\varphi}$ and $\widetilde{s} = \hat{s}$. In addition, $\widetilde{\gamma_{LP}}$ around the specified values (φ and s) were less than 25 % of the maximum correlation value under non-scrambling, γ_{LP}.

Figures 10(a) and 10(b) show the magnification of 1000 sets of $\widetilde{\varphi}$ and $\widetilde{s}$ estimated by the POC of the SMD of the template with the SMD of the query (head) and with the SMD of the query (liver), respectively, where $\varphi = 10$ and $s = 1.05$. Figures 10(c) and 10(d) show the magnification of 1000 sets of $\widetilde{\varphi}$ and $\widetilde{s}$ estimated

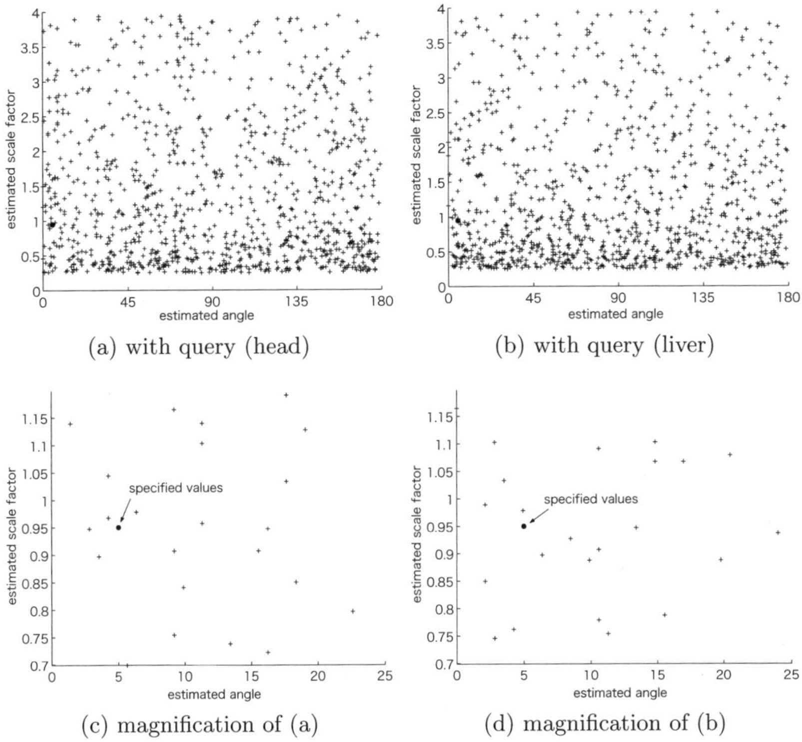

Fig. 9. Effectiveness of preventing illegal image matching ($\varphi = 5$ and $s = 0.95$). A total of 1000 different key sequences are used. The '+' plots denote that $\widetilde{\gamma_{LP}}$ is greater than or equal to 10% of γ_{LP} and less than 25% of γ_{LP}. (a) 1000 sets of $\widetilde{\varphi}$ and $\widetilde{s}$ estimated by the POC of the SMD of the template with the SMD of the query (head). (b) 1000 sets of $\widetilde{\varphi}$ and $\widetilde{s}$ estimated by the POC of the SMD of the template with the SMD of the query (liver). (c) Magnification of (a). (d) Magnification of (b).

by POC of the SMD of the template with the SMD of the query (head) and with the SMD of the query (liver), respectively, where $\varphi = 0$ and $s = 1$.

The histograms of $\widetilde{\varphi}$ and $\widetilde{s}$ in Figs. 9(a), 10(a), and 10(c) are shown in Figs 11(a), 11(b), and 11(c), respectively. When $\varphi = 5$, the mean and variance of the estimated rotation angle are 91.6 degrees and 2817.5, respectively. When $s = 0.95$, the mean and variance of the estimated scale factor are 1.41 and 1.0869, respectively. When $\varphi = 10$, the mean and variance of estimated rotation angle were 90.0 degrees and 2709.6, respectively. When $s = 1.05$, the mean and variance of estimated scale factor are 1.34 and 0.9972, respectively. When $\varphi = 0$, the mean and variance of the estimated rotation angle are 101.4 degrees and 2625.5, respectively. When $s = 1$, the mean and variance of the estimated scale factor are 1.30 and 0.9436, respectively. From these results, the mean and variance resemble the other mean and variance, and have no outstanding

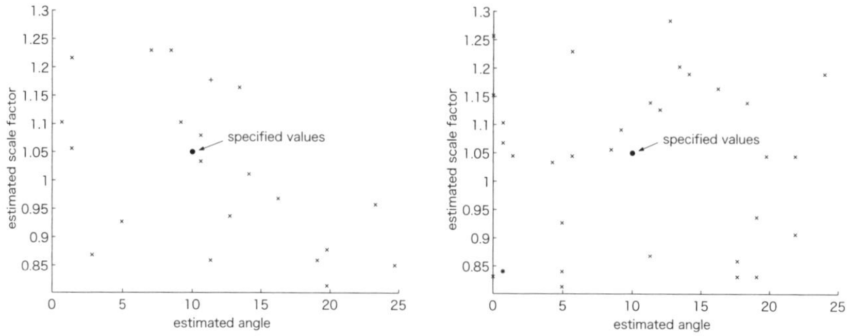

(a) with query (head) ($\varphi = 10,\ s = 1.05$) (b) with query (liver) ($\varphi = 10,\ s = 1.05$)

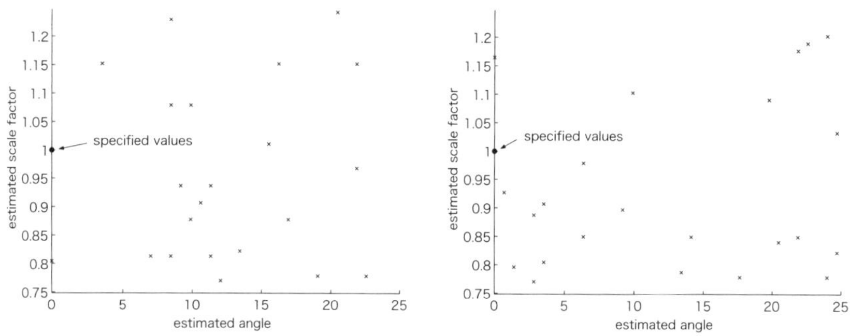

(c) with query (head) ($\varphi = 0,\ s = 1$) (d) with query (liver) ($\varphi = 0,\ s = 1$)

Fig. 10. Effectiveness of preventing illegal image matching ($\varphi = 10,\ s = 1.05$ and $\varphi = 0,\ s = 1$). A total of 1000 different key sequences are used. The 'x' plots denote that $\widetilde{\gamma_{LP}}$ is less than 10% of γ_{LP}. The '+' plots denote that $\widetilde{\gamma_{LP}}$ is greater than or equal to 10% of γ_{LP} and less than 25% of γ_{LP}. (a) Magnification of 1000 sets of $\widetilde{\varphi}$ and $\widetilde{s}$ estimated by the POC between the SMD of the template and the SMD of the query (head) ($\varphi = 10,\ s = 1.05$). (b) Magnification of 1000 sets of $\widetilde{\varphi}$ and $\widetilde{s}$ estimated by the POC between the SMD of the template and the SMD of the query (liver) ($\varphi = 10,\ s = 1.05$). (c) Magnification of 1000 sets of $\widetilde{\varphi}$ and $\widetilde{s}$ estimated by the POC between the SMD of the template and the SMD of the query (head) ($\varphi = 0,\ s = 1$). (d) Magnification of 1000 sets of $\widetilde{\varphi}$ and $\widetilde{s}$ estimated by the POC between the SMD of the template and the SMD of the query (liver) ($\varphi = 0,\ s = 1$).

characteristic. Therefore, it is difficult to deduce the template by POC using local images. We can confirm the effectiveness of preventing illegal image matching of the proposed method.

4.3 Histogram of the DFT Magnitude

Figure 12 shows three histograms for the process of generating SMD. The intensity is normalized. Figure 12(a) shows the histogram of the DFT magnitude of the image shown in Fig. 6(a). Figure 12(b) shows the histogram of the log-polar image mapped from 12(a). The histogram is changed by log-polar mapping, in which

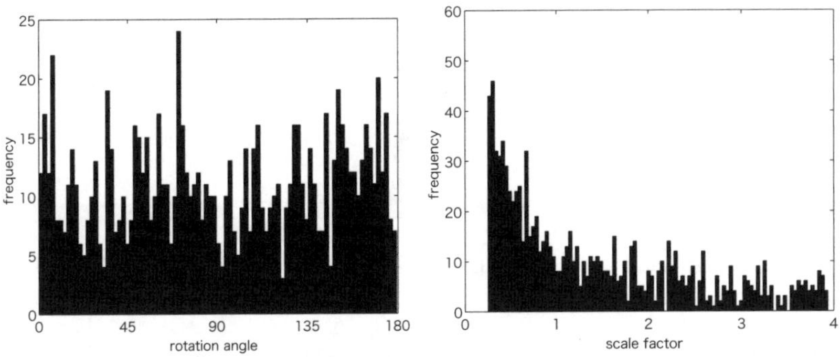

(a) $\varphi = 5$ and $s = 0.95$

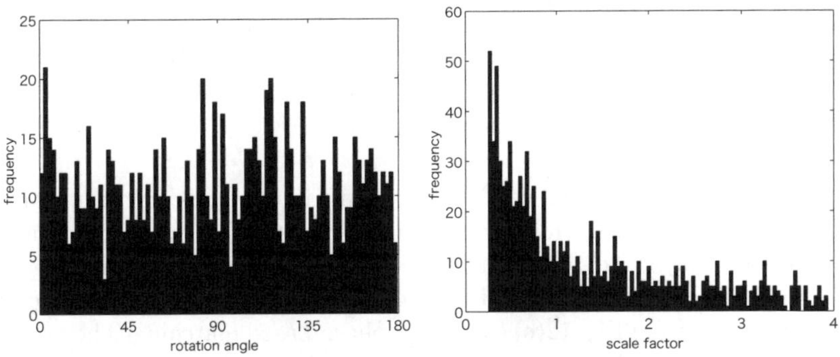

(b) $\varphi = 10$ and $s = 1.05$

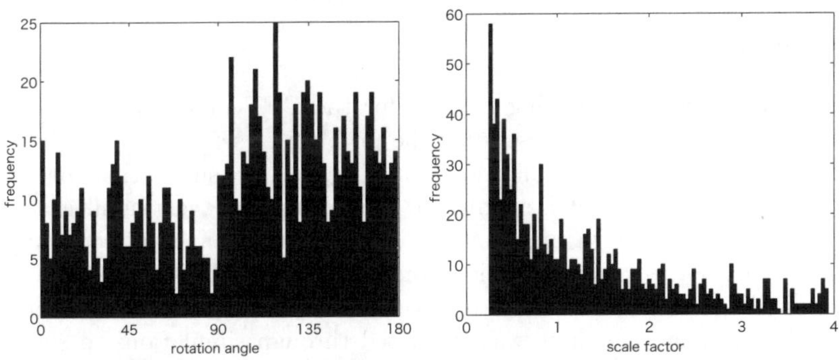

(c) $\varphi = 0$ and $s = 1$

Fig. 11. Histograms of $\widetilde{\varphi}$ and $\widetilde{s}$ estimated by the POC between the SMD of the template and the SMD of the query (head). (a) $\varphi = 5$ and $s = 0.95$. The mean and variance of the estimated rotation angle are 91.6 degrees and 2817.5, respectively. The mean and variance of the estimated scale factor are 1.41 and 1.0869, respectively. (b) $\varphi = 10$ and $s = 1.05$. The mean and variance of estimated rotation angle are 90.0 degrees and 2709.6, respectively. The mean and variance of estimated scale factor are 1.34 and 0.9972, respectively. (c) $\varphi = 0$ and $s = 1$. The mean and variance of the estimated rotation angle are 101.4 degrees and 2625.5, respectively. The mean and variance of the estimated scale factor are 1.30 and 0.9436, respectively.

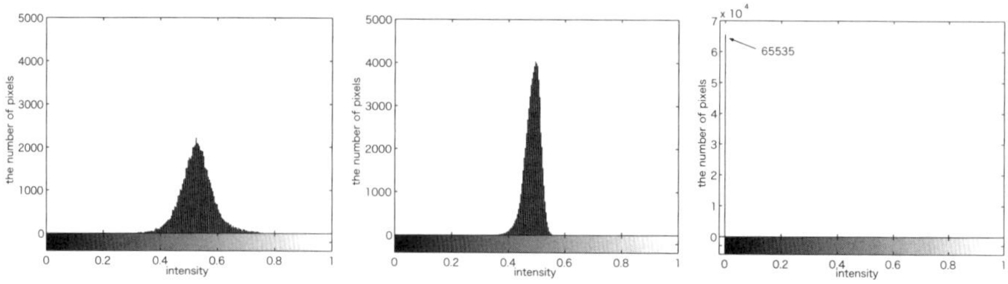

(a) DFT magnitude (b) Log-polar image (c) Inverse DFT of the absolute value of the SMD

Fig. 12. Histograms for the process of generating SMD. The intensity is normalized. (a) DFT magnitude of the template. (b) Log-polar image. When DFT magnitude is mapped into a log-polar image, the histogram is changed due to interpolation and unused points. (c) Inverse DFT of the absolute value of the SMD. Since the SMD is generated from the phase information of the log-polar image, it is difficult to deduce (a) from (c).

interpolation is performed and a number of points in the DFT-magnitude are not used. Figure 12(c) shows the histogram of the inverse DFT of the absolute value of the SMD. Since the SMD is generated from the phase information of the log-polar image, the characteristics of the DFT magnitude is hidden, and it is difficult to deduce Fig. 12(a) from Fig. 12(c) except for phase-based matching. The proposed scrambling is confirmed to protect the DFT magnitude of an image.

5 Conclusion

We have proposed a scrambling method for the DFT magnitude and an image matching system. After describing the problem of scrambling for the DFT magnitude by direct DFT magnitude scrambling, we have shown that the scrambling of the transformed DFT magnitude is effective in preventing illegal image matching. We have shown mathematically that POC can be directly applied to images in the proposed scrambled domain and that the same values under non-scrambling are obtained from the proposed scrambled domain. The prevention of illegal image matching was evaluated through simulations to show the effectiveness of the proposed method.

References

1. Knapp, C.H., Carter, G.C.: The Generalized Correlation Method for Estimation of Time Delay. IEEE Trans. Acoust., Speech, Signal Process. ASSP-24(4), 320–327 (1976)
2. Kuglin, C.D., Hines, D.C.: The Phase Correlation Image Alignment Method. In: Proc. Int. Conf. Cybernetics and Society, pp. 163–165 (1975)
3. Chen, Q., Defrise, M., Deconinck, F.: Symmetric Phase-only Matched Filtering of Fourier-Mellin Transforms for Image Registration and Recognition. IEEE Trans. Pattern Anal. Mach. Intell. 16(2), 1156–1168 (1994)

4. Thévenaz, P., Ruttimann, U.E., Unser, M.: A Pyramidal Approach to Subpixel Registration Based on Intensity. IEEE Trans. Image Process. 7(1), 27–41 (1998)
5. Foroosh, H., Zerubia, J., Berthod, M.: Extension of Phase Correlation to Sub-pixel Registration. IEEE Trans. Image Process. 11(3), 188–200 (2002)
6. Hoge, W.S.: A Subspace Identification Extension to the Phase Correlation Method. IEEE Trans. Med. Imag. 22(2), 277–280 (2003)
7. Foroosh, H., Balci, M.: Sub-pixel Registration and Estimation of Local Shifts Directly in the Fourier Domain. In: Proc. IEEE Int. Conf. Image Process. vol. 3, pp. 1915–1918 (2004)
8. Balci, M., Foroosh, H.: Subpixel Estimation of Shifts Directly in the Fourier Domain. IEEE Trans. Image Process. 15(7), 1965–1972 (2006)
9. Takita, K., Aoki, T., Sasaki, Y., Higuchi, T., Kobayashi, K.: High-accuracy Subpixel Image Registration Based on Phase-Only Correlation. IEICE Trans. Fundamentals E86-A(8), 1925–1934 (2003)
10. Ito, K., Nakajima, H., Kobayashi, K., Aoki, T., Higuchi, T.: A Fingerprint Matching Algorithm Using Phase-Only Correlation. IEICE Trans. Fundamentals E87-A(3), 682–691 (2004)
11. Ito, K., Nikaido, A., Aoki, T., Kosuge, E., Kawamata, R., Kashima, I.: A Dental Radiograph Recognition System Using Phase-Only Correlation for Human Identification. IEICE Trans. Fundamentals E91-A(1), 298–305 (2008)
12. Ito, K., Aoki, T., Nakajima, H., Kobayashi, K., Higuchi, T.: A Palmprint Recognition Algorithm Using Phase-Only Correlation. IEICE Trans. Fundamentals E91-A(4), 1023–1030 (2008)
13. Miyazawa, K., Ito, K., Aoki, T., Kobayashi, K., Nakajima, H.: An Effective Approach for Iris Recognition Using Phase-based Image Matching. IEEE Trans. Pattern Anal. Mach. Intell. 30(10), 1741–1756 (2008)
14. Jain, A.K., Ross, A., Pankanti, S.: Biometrics: A Tool for Information Security. IEEE Trans. Inf. Forensics Security 1(2), 125–143 (2006)
15. Fujiyoshi, M., Saitou, W., Watanabe, O., Kiya, H.: Hierarchical Encryption of Multimedia Contents for Access Control. In: Proc. IEEE Int. Conf. Image Process., pp. 1977–1980 (2006)
16. Kuroiwa, K., Fujiyoshi, M., Kiya, H.: Codestream Domain Scrambling of Moving Objects Based on DCT Sign-Only Correlation for Motion JPEG Movies. In: Proc. IEEE Int. Conf. Image Process., vol. V, pp. 157–160 (2007)
17. Bianchi, T., Piva, A., Barni, M.: Implementing the Discrete Fourier Transform in the Encrypted Domain. In: Proc. IEEE Int. Conf. Acoust., Speech Signal Process., pp. 1757–1760 (2008)
18. Bianchi, T., Piva, A., Barni, M.: Comparison of Different FFT Implementations in the Encrypted Domain. In: Proc. 16th European Signal Process. Conf. (2008)
19. Kiya, H., Ito, I.: Image Matching between Scrambled Images for Secure Data Management. In: Proc. 16th European Signal Process. Conf. (2008)
20. Ito, I., Kiya, H.: A New Class of Image Registration for Guaranteeing Secure Data Management. In: Proc. IEEE Int. Conf. Image Process., pp. 269–272 (2008)
21. Ito, I., Kiya, H.: DCT Sign-Only Correlation with Application to Image Matching and the Relationship with Phase-Only Correlation. In: Proc. IEEE Int. Conf. Acoust., Speech Signal Process., vol. 1, pp. 1237–1240 (2007)
22. Schneier, B.: Applied Cryptography. John Wiley & Sons, Inc., Chichester (1996)
23. Ito, I., Kiya, H.: Phase scrambling for blind image matching. In: Proc. IEEE Int. Conf. Acoustics, Speech and Signal Processing, pp. 1521–1524 (2009)

A Comprehensive Study of Visual Cryptography

Jonathan Weir and WeiQi Yan

Queen's University Belfast, Belfast, BT7 1NN, UK

Abstract. Visual cryptography (VC) is a powerful technique that combines the notions of perfect ciphers and secret sharing in cryptography with that of raster graphics. VC takes a binary image (the secret) and divides it into two or more pieces known as shares. When the shares are printed on transparencies and then superimposed, the secret can be recovered. No computer participation is required, thus demonstrating one of the distinguishing features of VC. VC is a unique technique in the sense that the encrypted message can be decrypted directly by the human visual system (HVS). In this survey, we will summarize the latest developments of visual cryptography since its inception in 1994, introduce the main research topics in this area and outline the current problems and possible solutions. Directions and trends for future VC work shall also be examined along with possible VC applications.

1 Introduction

Visual cryptography is a powerful technique which combines the notions of perfect ciphers and secret sharing in cryptography with that of raster graphics. A binary image can be divided into shares which can be stacked together to approximately recover the original image. A secret sharing scheme enables distribution of a secret amongst n parties, such that only predefined authorized sets will be able to reconstruct the secret. The secret, in terms of visual cryptography can be reconstructed visually by superimposing shares.

Visual cryptography allows the transmission of visual information and many aspects of this area are covered, including its inception to the current techniques being employed and actively researched today. This survey covers the progress of VC, along with the current trends and the various applications for VC.

Having the ability to hide information such as personal details is very desirable. When the data is hidden within separate images (known as shares), it is completely unrecognizable. While the shares are separate, the data is completely incoherent. Each image holds different pieces of the data and when they are brought together, the secret can be recovered easily. They each rely on one another in order to obtain the decrypted information. There should be no way that anyone could decipher the information contained within any of the shares. When the shares are brought together, deciphering is possible when the shares are placed over one another. At this point, the information becomes instantly available. No computational power is required at all in order to decrypt the information. All decryption is performed by the human visual system (HVS). This kind of problem is formally referred to as a secret sharing problem.

Y.Q. Shi (Ed.): Transactions on DHMS V, LNCS 6010, pp. 70–105, 2010.

Secret sharing using visual cryptography is different from typical cryptographic secret sharing. The latter allows each party to keep a portion of the secret and provides a way to know at least part of the secret, while the former strictly prohibits it. Encryption using multiple keys is a possible solution. However this solution requires a large number of keys, therefore the management of such a scheme becomes troublesome, as demonstrated by Shamir.

In 1979, Adi Shamir published an article titled "How to share a secret" [1]. In this article, the following example was used to describe a typical secret sharing problem:

> "Eleven scientists are working on a secret project. They wish to lock up the documents in a cabinet so that the cabinet can be opened if and only if six or more of the scientists are present. What is the smallest number of locks needed? What is the smallest number of keys to the locks each scientist must carry?
>
> ...
>
> The minimal solution uses 462 locks and 252 keys per scientist."

In the paper, Shamir generalized the above problem and formulated the definition of (k, n)-threshold scheme. The definition can be explained as follows: Let D be the secret to be shared among n parties. A (k, n)-threshold scheme is a way to divide D into n pieces $D_1, \cdots, D_n$ that satisfies the conditions:

1. Knowledge of any k or more D_i pieces makes D easily computable;
2. Knowledge of any $k-1$ or fewer D_i pieces leaves D completely undetermined (in the sense that all its possible values are equally likely).

Visual cryptography is a new type of cryptographic scheme that focuses on solving this problem of secret sharing. Visual cryptography uses the idea of hiding secrets within images. These images are encoded into multiple shares and later decoded without any computation. This decoding is as simple as superimposing transparencies, which allows the secret to be recovered.

Visual cryptography is a desirable scheme as it embodies both the idea of perfect secrecy (using a one time pad) and a very simple mechanism for decrypting/decoding the secret. The interesting feature about visual cryptography is that it is perfectly secure. There is a simple analogy from one time padding to visual cryptography. If we consider the current popular cryptographic schemes, which are usually only conditionally secure, we can see that this is the second critical advantage of visual cryptography over other cryptographic schemes.

This survey is organized as follows: Section 2 details the very first form of visual cryptography and elaborates on the current work still being done in this area, specifically the most recent improvements. In general, these schemes primarily deal with binary images and noisy random shares. Extended forms of VC are also presented within this section which attempt to alleviate the suspicion of encryption within the shares. Section 3 concentrates on cheating prevention within VC along with cheating immune VC schemes. These schemes attempt to have some type of authentication or verification method which gives some clue as to the real hidden secret within a given set of shares. Grayscale, halftone and colour halftone images used in conjunction with visual cryptography are set forth in Section 4. Section 5 elaborates on multiple secret sharing, which involves sharing two or more secrets, typically within a set of two shares. Various applications of visual cryptography are analysed in Section 6 and the summary and future work are discussed within Section 7, along with the final conclusion.

2 Traditional Visual Cryptography

2.1 Basic Visual Cryptography

Image sharing is a subset of secret sharing because it acts as a special approach to the general secret sharing problem. The secrets in this case are concealed images. Each secret is treated as a number, this allows a specific encoding scheme supplied for each source of the secrets. Without the problem of inverse conversions, the digits may not be interpreted correctly to represent the true meaning of the secret.

Image sharing defines a scheme which is identical to that of general secret sharing. In (k, n) image sharing, the image that carries the secret is split up into n pieces (known as shares) and the decryption is totally unsuccessful unless at least k pieces are collected and superimposed.

Visual cryptography was originally invented and pioneered by Moni Naor and Adi Shamir in 1994 at the Eurocrypt conference. Visual cryptography is "a new type of cryptographic scheme, which can decode concealed images without any cryptographic computation" [2]. As the name suggests, visual cryptography is related to the human visual system. When the k shares are stacked together, the human eyes do the decryption. This allows anyone to use the system without any knowledge of cryptography and without performing any computations whatsoever. This is another advantage of visual cryptography over the other popular conditionally secure cryptography schemes. The mechanism is very secure and very easily implemented. An electronic secret can be shared directly, alternatively the secrets can be printed out onto transparencies and superimposed, revealing the secret.

Naor and Shamir's initial implementation assumes that the image or message is a collection of black and white pixels, each pixel is handled individually and it should be noted that the white pixel represents the transparent colour. One disadvantage of this is that the decryption process is lossy, the area that suffers due to this is the contrast. Contrast is very important within visual cryptography because it determines the clarity of the recovered secret by the human visual system. The relative difference in Hamming weight between the representation of white and black pixels signify the loss in contrast of the recovered secret. The Hamming weight is explained further at a later stage. Newer schemes that are discussed later deal with grayscale and colour images which attempt to minimize the loss in contrast [3] by using digital halftoning. Halftoning allows a continuous tone image, which may be made up from an infite range of colours or grays to be represented as a binary image. Varying dot sizes and the distance between those dots create an optical illusion. It is this illusion which allows the human eye to blend these dots making the halftone image appear as a continuous tone image. Due to the fact that digital halftoning is a lossy process in itself [4], it is impossible to fully reconstruct the original secret image.

The encryption problem is expressed as a k out of n secret sharing problem. Given the image or message, n transparencies are generated so that the original image (message) is visible if any k of them are stacked together. The image remains hidden if fewer than k transparencies are stacked together.

Each pixel appears within n modified versions (known as shares) per transparency. The shares are a collection of m black and white sub-pixels arranged closely together. The structure can be described as an $n \times m$ Boolean matrix S. The structure of S can be described thus: $S = (s_{ij})_{m \times n}$ where $s_{ij} = 1$ or 0 *i.f.f.* the jth sub-pixel of the ith share is black or white.

The important parameters of the scheme are:

1. m, the number of pixels in a share. This represents the loss in resolution from the original image to the recovered one.
2. α, the relative difference in the weight between the combined shares that come from a white and black pixel in the original image, i.e., the loss in contrast.
3. γ, the size of the collection of C_0 and C_1. C_0 refers to the sub-pixel patterns in the shares for a white pixel and C_1 refers to the sub-pixel patterns in the shares for a black pixel.

The Hamming weight $H(V)$ of the ORed m-vector V is interpreted by the visual system as follows:

A black pixel is interpreted if $H(V) \leq d$ and white if $H(V) < d - \alpha m$ for some fixed threshold $1 \leq d \leq m$ and a relative difference $\alpha > 0$.

The construction of the shares can be clearly illustrated by a 2 out of 2 visual cryptography scheme (commonly known as $(2,2)$-VCS). The following collections of 2×2 matrices are defined:

$C_0 = \{$all the matrices obtained by permuting the columns of $\begin{bmatrix} 1\,1\,0\,0 \\ 1\,1\,0\,0 \end{bmatrix}\}$

$C_1 = \{$all the matrices obtained by permuting the columns of $\begin{bmatrix} 1\,1\,0\,0 \\ 0\,0\,1\,1 \end{bmatrix}\}$

Due to this pixel expansion, one pixel from the original image gets expanded into four pixels. The shares can be generated in the following manner:

1. If the pixel of the original binary image is white, randomly pick the same pattern of four pixels for both shares.
2. If the pixel of the original image is black, pick a complementary pair of patterns, i.e., the patterns from the same column in Figure 1.

When the transparencies are superimposed and the sub-pixels are correctly aligned, the black pixels in the combined shares are represented by the Boolean OR of the rows in the matrix. The pixels can be arranged in various ways

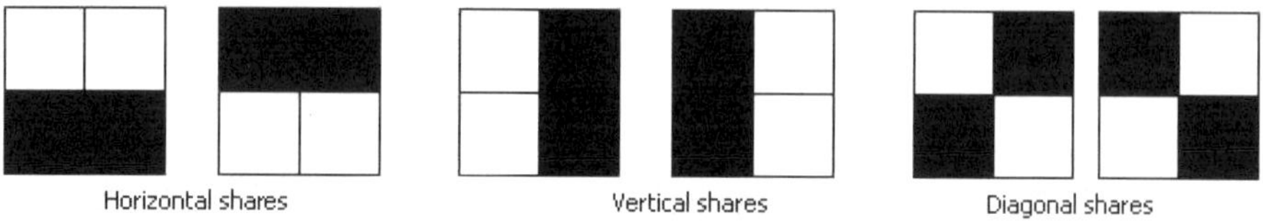

Fig. 1. The various types of pixel patterns used when creating VC shares

within the matrix. Visual representation of the different types of share patterns is present in Figure 1.

Because the individual shares give no clue into whether a specific pixel is black or white it becomes impossible to decrypt the shares, no matter how much computational power is available.

Below in Figure 2, the implementation and results of (2, 2)-VCS basic visual cryptography are shown. It displays the secret image, the two shares that are generated and the recovery of the secret after superimposing share one and share two.

(a) Secret Image (108 × 121) (b) Share 1, S_1 (216 × 242) (c) Share 2, S_2 (216 × 242) (d) Restored image, $S_1 + S_2$ (216 × 242)

Fig. 2. The results of a traditional visual cryptography scheme

2.2 Extended Visual Cryptography

An extended visual cryptography scheme (EVCS) proposed by Ateniese et al. [5] is based on an access structure which contains two types of sets, a qualified access structure Γ_{Qual} and a forbidden access structure Γ_{Forb} in a set of n participants. The technique encodes the participants in that, if any set, which is a member of the qualified access structure, are superimposed, then the secret message is revealed. However, for any set which is a member of the forbidden access structure and has no information on the shared secret, this means no useful information can be gleaned from stacking the participants. The main difference between basic visual cryptography and extended visual cryptography is that a recognizable image can be viewed on each of the shares; once the shares have been superimposed (provided they are part of the qualified access structure), the image on the shares will disappear and the secret message will be visible.

Extended visual cryptography schemes allow the construction of visual secret sharing schemes within which the shares are meaningful as opposed to having random noise on the shares. After the sets of shares are superimposed, this meaningful information disappears and the secret is recovered. This is the basis for the extended form of visual cryptography.

With EVCS, the first n shares need to be images of something like a car, boat or dog, some form of meaningful information. The secret message or image is normally the last to be dealt with $(n+1)$. This requires a technique that has to take into consideration the colour of the pixel in the secret image we want to obtain, so when the n shares are superimposed, their individual images disappear and the secret image can be seen. In general, this can be denoted by $C_c^{c_1 \cdots c_n}$ with $c, c_1, \cdots, c_n \in \{b, w\}$, the collection of matrices from which we can choose a matrix to determine the shares, given c_i being the colour of the ith innocent image and c being the colour of the secret image. In order to implement this scheme, 2^n pairs of such collections, one for each possible combination of white and black pixels in the n original images need to be generated.

It is assumed that no information is known on the pixel values of the original image that is being hidden. The only thing that is known is that the pixels can be black or white. No probability distribution is known about the pixels. There is no way to tell if a black pixel is more likely to occur than a white pixel. Three conditions must be met when it comes to encrypting the images. Firstly, images that belong to the qualified set access structure, should, when superimposed, reveal the secret image. Secondly, by inspecting the shares, no hint should be available about what secret is hidden within the shares. Finally, the image within the shares should not be altered in anyway, that is, after the n original images have been encoded, they should still be recognizable by the user.

The simplest example is a (2, 2)-EVCS problem. The collections $C_c^{c_1, c_2}$ are obtained by permuting the columns of the following matrices:

$$S_w^{ww} = \begin{bmatrix} 1\,0\,0\,1 \\ 1\,0\,0\,0 \end{bmatrix} \quad \textit{and} \quad S_b^{ww} = \begin{bmatrix} 1\,0\,0\,1 \\ 0\,1\,1\,0 \end{bmatrix} \tag{1}$$

$$S_w^{wb} = \begin{bmatrix} 1\,0\,0\,1 \\ 1\,0\,1\,1 \end{bmatrix} \quad \textit{and} \quad S_b^{ww} = \begin{bmatrix} 1\,0\,0\,1 \\ 0\,1\,1\,1 \end{bmatrix} \tag{2}$$

$$S_w^{bw} = \begin{bmatrix} 1\,0\,1\,1 \\ 1\,0\,1\,0 \end{bmatrix} \quad \textit{and} \quad S_b^{bw} = \begin{bmatrix} 1\,0\,1\,1 \\ 0\,1\,1\,0 \end{bmatrix} \tag{3}$$

$$S_w^{bb} = \begin{bmatrix} 1\,0\,1\,1 \\ 1\,0\,1\,1 \end{bmatrix} \quad \textit{and} \quad S_b^{bb} = \begin{bmatrix} 1\,0\,1\,1 \\ 0\,1\,1\,1 \end{bmatrix} \tag{4}$$

It can also be verified that for a (2, 2)-EVCS, the contrast values achieved for both shares and the recovered secret image are all $\frac{1}{4}$.

Figure 3 provides an example of a (2, 2)-EVCS. As can be seen from the figure, two meaningful shares are generated from the base images. During this share creation, the secret is encoded between each of the shares. After superimposing

(a) Base image 1 (271 × 69).

(b) Base image 2 (271 × 69).

(c) Secret (271 × 69).

(d) Extended share 1, ES_1 (542 × 138).

(e) Extended share 2, ES_2 (542 × 138).

(f) Recovered secret ES_1 + ES_2 (542 × 138).

Fig. 3. The results of an extended visual cryptography scheme

each share, the secret is completely recovered while each shares meaningful information disappears.

In order to use this extended visual cryptography scheme, a general construction needs to be defined. Ateniese et al. [5] have devised a mechanism by which we can generate the shares for the scheme.

A stronger security model for EVCS is one in which the shares associated with a forbidden subset can be inspected by the user, meaning that the secret image will still remain totally hidden even if all n shares are previously known by the user. A systematic approach to fully address a general (k, n) problem was also proposed [6].

For each set of access structures, let $P = \{1, \cdots, n\}$ represent the set of elements called participants, and let 2^P denote the set of all subsets of P. Let $\Gamma_{Qual}/\Gamma_{Forb}$ be the collection of qualified / forbidden sets. The pair is called the access structure of the scheme. Any qualified set can recover the shared image by stacking its participants transparencies, while any forbidden set has no information on the shared image. This extension generalizes the original secret sharing problem by [2]. In [6], the authors propose a new technique to realize (k, n)-VCS, which is better with respect to the pixel expansion than the one proposed by Naor and Shamir. Schemes for improving the contract are discussed later.

Improving the shares quality [7] to that of a photo realistic picture has also been examined within extended visual cryptography. This is achieved using gray subpixels rather than black and white pixels in the form of halftoning.

2.3 Size Invariant Visual Cryptography

One of the first papers to consider image size invariant VC was proposed by Ito et al. [8]. As previously described, traditional visual cryptography schemes employ pixel expansion, although many have worked on how to improve this [9].

Ito's scheme [8] removes the need for this pixel expansion. The scheme uses the traditional (k, n) scheme where m (the number of subpixels in a shared pixel) is equal to one. The structure of this scheme is described by a Boolean n-vector $\mathbf{V} = [v_1, \cdots, v_n]^T$, where v_i represents the colour of the pixel in the i-th shared image. If $v_i = 1$ then the pixel is black, otherwise, if $v_i = 0$ then the pixel is white. To reconstruct the secret, traditional ORing is applied to the pixels in $\mathbf{V}$. The recovered secret can be viewed as the difference of probabilities with which a black pixel in the reconstructed image is generated from a white and black pixel in the secret image. As with traditional visual cryptography, $n \times m$ sets of matrices need to be defined for the scheme:

$$C_0 = \{\text{all the matrices obtained by permuting the columns of } \begin{bmatrix} 1 & 0 & 0 \cdots 0 \\ 1 & 0 & 0 \cdots 0 \\ \cdots & & \\ 1 & 0 & 0 \cdots 0 \end{bmatrix}\}$$

$$C_1 = \{\text{all the matrices obtained by permuting the columns of } \begin{bmatrix} 1 & 0 & 0 \cdots 0 \\ 0 & 1 & 0 \cdots 0 \\ \cdots & & \\ 0 & 0 & 0 \cdots 1 \end{bmatrix}\}$$

Because this scheme uses no pixel expansion, m is always equal to one and n is based on the type of scheme being used, for example a $(2, 3)$ scheme, $n = 3$. The most important part of any visual secret sharing scheme is the contrast. The lower the contrast, the harder it is to visually recover the secret. The contrast for this scheme is defined as follows: $\beta = |p_0 - p_1|$, where p_0 and p_1 are the probabilities with which a black pixel on the reconstructed image is generated from a white and black pixel on the secret image.

Using the defined sets of matrices C_0 and C_1, and a contrast $\beta = \frac{1}{3}$, $n \times m$ Boolean matrices S^0 and S^1 are chosen at random from C_0 and C_1, respectively:

$$S_0 = \begin{bmatrix} 1\,0\,0 \\ 1\,0\,0 \\ 1\,0\,0 \end{bmatrix}, S_1 = \begin{bmatrix} 1\,0\,0 \\ 0\,1\,0 \\ 0\,0\,1 \end{bmatrix} \tag{5}$$

To share a white pixel, one of the columns in S_0 is chosen and to share a black pixel, one of the columns in S_1 is chosen. This chosen column vector $\mathbf{V} = [v_1, \cdots, v_n]^T$ defines the colour of each pixel in the corresponding shared image. Each v_i is interpreted as black if $v_i = 1$ and as white if $v_i = 0$. Sharing a black pixel for example, one column is chosen at random in S^1, resulting in the following vector:

$$\mathbf{V} = \begin{bmatrix} 0 \\ 1 \\ 0 \end{bmatrix} \tag{6}$$

Therefore, the i-th element determines the colour of the pixels in the i-th shared image, thus in this (2,3) example, v_1 is white in the first shared image, v_2 is black in the second shared image and in the third shared image, v_3 is white.

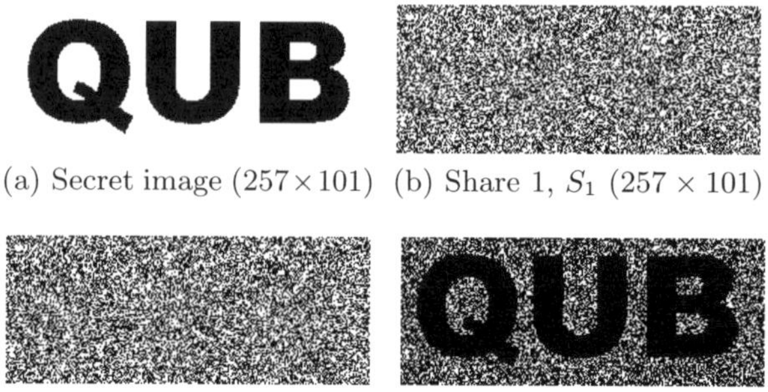

(a) Secret image (257×101) (b) Share 1, S_1 (257 × 101)

(c) Share 2, S_2 (257 × 101) (d) Recovered secret, S_1+S_2 (257 × 101)

Fig. 4. Result of a size invariant visual cryptography scheme

This process is repeated for all pixels in the secret image resulting in the final set of shares. Figure 4 provides an example based on the (2,2) scheme.

A probabilistic method to deal with size invariant shares is proposed in [10] in which the frequency of white pixels is used to show the contrast of the recovered image. The scheme is non-expansible and can be easily implemented on the basis of conventional visual secret sharing (VSS) schemes. The term non-expansible means that the sizes of the original image and shadows are the same.

As discussed previously, many schemes presented so far involve pixel expansion. Researchers have examined this area and found it to be a worthwhile research topic [11,12]. This leads on to a related topic within size invariant schemes, namely, aspect ratio.

Aspect ratio invariant secret sharing is presented by Yang and Chen [13]. This aspect ratio invariant secret sharing scheme dramatically reduces the number of extra subpixels needed in order to construct the secret. This results in smaller shares, closer to the size of the original secret while also maintaining the aspect ratio, thus avoiding distortion when reconstructing the secret. Alternatively this problem can be examined from the opposite end, trading overall share size and contrast. A size-adjustable scheme is presented [14] that allows the user to choose an appropriate share size that is practical for the current use of the shares. If quality and contrast matter then the size of the shares will increase, whereas the opposite can happen if these things are not overly important for a user's particular application.

Yang and Chen [15] further progress this research by generalizing the aspect ratio invariant problem. To achieve the same relative position between two square blocks, and to avoid distortion, the re-sampling method in image scaling [16,17] is used.

2.4 Quality Evaluation

From its inception in 1994, VC remains an important research topic. Even this very basic form of VC is still being researched and improved upon. Specific improvements that are worth a mention include the size invariant forms of visual cryptography. More specifically, the schemes which minimize pixel expansion and also increase the overall contrast, which results in very clear secret recovery. The size adjustable scheme discussed above, which allows the user to specify what size of shares to generate is very interesting work. This allows for a user defined tradeoff between quality and portability of shares. This increases the potential for VC once again, rather than being restricted on a specific scheme which only allows for a certain type of quality. Application dependant forms of visual cryptography would be a worthwhile area of further research.

Optimal contrast secret sharing schemes in visual cryptography have been discussed at length because it is an extremely important evaluation metric for any scheme. This is mainly due to how the overall contrast affects the quality of the recovered secret.

Hofmeister et al. [18] present a linear solution to the optimal contrast problem. An approach based on coding theory helps to provide an optimal tradeoff between the contrast and the number of subpixels. Optimal $(2, n)$-schemes are examined in terms of contrast related to the Hamming distance, as well as the subpixel tradeoff required for these optimal schemes. A general scheme for k is also presented which encapsulates a contrast-optimal (k, n)-scheme, where a linear program for calculating the maximum contrast is presented. Solving this linear program results in the optimal achievable contrast in any (k, n)-scheme. Table 1 (taken from Hofmeister) displays some of these calculated optimal contrast solutions.

Table 1. Computed values of a (k, n)-scheme for the optimal contrast solution

$k \backslash n$	2	3	4	5	6	...	10	...	50	...	100
2	1/2	1/3	1/3	3/10	3/10		5/18		25/98		25/99
3		1/4	1/6	1/8	1/10		1/12		13/196		625/9702
4			1/8	1/15	1/18		1/35		1161/65800		425/25608

A possible option for improving the efficiency of VC is to use the XOR operation [19]. This method will not allow traditional stacking of the shares on transparencies but it will improve the overall share quality. The scheme has favourable properties, such as, good resolution and high contrast. It can be applied to colour images as well.

An interesting scheme presented within [20] outlines the procedure for previewing the secret hidden within two shares. The main idea behind this is that if the shares are damaged in some way, recovering the secret using the computationally intensive Lagrange polynomial method [21,22], can turn out to be a waste of time. Therefore, having the ability to check the shares prior to the perfect recover phase is important and can solve a lot of potential problems.

The downside to some of these basic forms of VC is that the shares potentially give away the fact that they are encrypted. Extended VC helps with this, producing meaningful shares which have the same pixel expansion as the original basic VC schemes, but in today's world of high quality imaging, a small minority of users would be dealing with binary images, so most users would not have a use for this in terms of high quality images. However, the use of these efficient basic schemes would provide a secure form of 2D barcodes.

3 Cheating Immune Visual Cryptography

Despite visual cryptography's secure nature, many researchers have experimented with the idea of cheating the system. Methods for cheating the basic VC schemes have been presented, along with techniques used for cheating extended VC schemes [23,24,25].

3.1 Authentication Methods

Prevention of cheating via authentication methods [24] have been proposed which focus on identification between two participants to help prevent any type of cheating taking place. Yang and Laih [25] presented two types of cheating prevention, one type used an online trust authority to perform the verification between the participants. The second type involved changing the VC scheme whereby the stacking of two shares reveals a verification image, however this method requires the addition of extra pixels in the secret.

Another cheating prevention scheme described by Horng et al. [23], whereby if an attacker knows the exact distribution of black and white pixels of each of the shares of honest participants then they will be able to successfully attack and cheat the scheme. Horng's method prevents the attacker from obtaining this distribution.

3.2 Cheat Prevention

Successfully cheating a VCS however, does not require knowledge of the distribution of black and white pixels. Hu and Tzeng [26] where able to present numerous cheating methods, each of which where capable of cheating Horng et al.'s cheating prevention scheme. Hu and Tzeng also present improvements on Yang and Laih's scheme and finally present their own cheating prevention scheme which attempts to minimize the overall additional pixels which may be required. No online trust authority is required and the verification of each image is different and confidential. The contrast is minimally changed and the cheating prevention scheme should apply to any VCS. Hu and Tzeng where also able to prove that both a malicious participant (**MP**), that is $\mathbf{MP} \in P$, and a malicious outsider (**MO**), $\mathbf{MO} \notin P$, can cheat in some circumstances.

The **MP** is able to construct a fake set of shares using his genuine share. After the fake share has been stacked on the genuine share, the fake secret can be viewed. The second cheating method involving an **MO** is capable of cheating the VC scheme without having any knowledge of any genuine shares. The **MO** firstly creates a set of fake shares based on the optimal $(2,2)$-VCS. Next, the fake shares are required to be resized to that of the original genuine shares size.

However, an assumption is to be made on the genuine shares size, namely that these shares where printed onto a standard size of paper, something like A4 or A3. Therefore, shares of those sizes are created, along with fractions of those sizes. Management of this type of scheme would prove to be problematic due to the number of potential shares created in order to have a set of the correct size required to cheat a specific scheme, but once that size is known, cheating is definitely possible as an **MO**.

3.3 A Traceable Model

A traceable model of visual cryptography [27] was also examined which also helps to deal with cheating. It deals with the scenario when a coalition of less than k traitors who stack their shares and publish the result so that other coalitions of the participants can illegally reveal the secret. In the traceable model, it is possible to trace the saboteurs with the aid of special markings. The constructions of traceable schemes for both (k, n) and (n, n) problems were also presented.

3.4 Quality Evaluation

Most notable improvements on cheating immune VC schemes have been presented within [26] which presents examples for traditional and extended schemes. The pixel expansion and contrast reduction are minimal and acceptable due to the overall improvements presented within [26].

The addition of an authentication method, whereby, each participant must verify every other participant is an important improvement. Even with this additional feature, the contrast does not drop significantly enough to rule out this scheme. The drop in contrast is very slight when compared to previous schemes.

Finally, even when some participants collaborate together in order to subvert the system, they cannot succeed. The overall quality and thought that has gone into this scheme is highly impressive and extremely useful.

4 Grayscale, Halftone and Colour Visual Cryptography

A brief introduction to halftoning and error diffusion techniques are given before the main VC schemes which use these technologies are presented. It is important to understand how these technologies work beforehand, as they are frequently used within many visual cryptography schemes.

Halftoning is a print and display technique that trades area for gray-level depth by partitioning an image into small areas in which pixels of different values are purposely arranged to reflect the tone density. There are three main factors that effect these arranged pixels or dot structure, namely, the screen frequency (the number of lines per inch), the dot shape (the shape of the dots as they increase in size from light to dark), and the screen angle (the orientation of lines relative to the positive horizontal axis) [4].

In conjunction, error diffusion techniques coincide with halftone technology. Error diffusion is an adaptive technique that quantizes each pixel according to the input pixel as well as its neighbors. Error diffusion forces total tone content to remain the same and attempts to localize the distribution of tone levels [28]. At each pixel, the errors from its preceding neighbours are added to the original pixel value. This modified value then has a threshold applied to it.

4.1 Grayscale and Halftone Visual Cryptography

This method of secret sharing expands on Naor and Shamir's original findings in the 2-out-of-2 secret sharing scheme. It also takes extended visual cryptography a step further. The halftoning technique that is used can be applied to colour and grayscale images. Halftoning simulates a continuous tone through the use of dots, varying either in size or in spacing [29]. Grayscale halftoning is discussed within this section. Section 4.2 details colour halftone visual cryptography.

Based on the idea of extended visual cryptography, Zhou et al. [30] set about improving these techniques by proposing halftone grayscale images which carry significant visual information. Traditional VC produces random patterns of dots with no visual meaning until the shares are superimposed. This raises the suspicion of data encryption. Halftoning attempts to alleviate this suspicion by having visually pleasing attributes. This means creating halftone shares that carry one piece of information, such as another image, while having the secret hidden until both shares are superimposed. This gives no indication that any encryption has been performed on both shares. This in itself drastically improves the security model for visual cryptography. Along with Zhou, [31,32,33] present novel techniques by which halftone images can be shared with significant visual meaning which have a higher quality than those presented within [34] by employing error diffusion techniques [4]. These error diffusion techniques spread the pixels as homogeneously as possible to achieve the improvements in the shares overall quality.

A halftone scheme [35] was proposed in which the quality of the shares is improved by using contrast enhancement techniques. However the problem with this scheme is that it is not perfectly secure.

By using a space-filling curve ordered dithering technique [36], grayscale images can be converted into an approximate binary image. This allows encryption and decryption of the gray-level images using traditional visual cryptography methods [37].

Further improvements made in this area where achieved by using better error diffusion techniques, the technique proposed in [32] satisfies the following 3 requirements: (i) a secret image should be a natural image, (ii) images that carry a secret image should be a high quality natural images and (iii) computational cost should be low. This technique is based on [38] which satisfies both (ii) and (iii) and in order to satisfy (i), introduces an additional feedback mechanism into the secret image embedding process in order to improve the quality of the visually decoded secret image. Methods described in [35,39] only satisfy part of the three requirements.

The method proposed by Myodo et al. [32] allows natural embedding of grayscale images. The quality of the superimposed image highly depends on its dynamic range and pixel density. The possible pixel density of the superimposed image can be defined as: $max(0, g'_1 + g'_2 - 1) < d_s < min(g'_1, g'_2)$, where g'_1 and g'_2 are pixel values of the dynamic-range-controlled input images and d_s is the pixel density of the superposed image that is estimated with the surrounding pixels. The equation indicates that $g'_1 = g'_2 = 0.5$ gives the widest dynamic range of the superimposed image. Therefore, pixel values of input images should be modified around 0.5 by reducing their dynamic range. Accordingly, each pixel value of a secret image should be restricted between 0 and 0.5. This provides the mechanism for allowing any grayscale natural image to be used as an input.

The next stage is embedding the grayscale secret image. Along with the conventional method of enhancing the images using a feedback mechanism, another feedback mechanism is proposed to the secret image embedding process to enhance the quality of the superimposed image. Outlined below are the details of this method.

The typical error diffusion data hiding process is extended and another new system is also added. The extension involves ANDing the temporary shares within the system. The pixel values of the second share are determined one by one during the embedding process. Therefore, this superimposing operation can only be performed on the processed area of the share. Then the proposed method estimates density of the temporary superimposed image. During this density calculation, a low-pass filter such as a Gaussian filter [17] is used.

In order to make the superimposed result closer to the secret image, the new component is introduced. This new process decides how the current density should be controlled, either made darker or brighter. This is controlled by the distance between the pixel values in the secret and the density. If the density is much lower than the pixel value, then the density becomes brighter in order to achieve the desired embedding of the secret. Overall, this improves the quality of the original grayscale secret image and the most advantageous part of the new mechanism is that no iteration is required in the same way as the method described in [38].

The conventional method described in [38] uses an error diffusion halftoning technique [40] which works as follows: two grayscale images are used for input along with a secret image. Typically, the secret image cannot be used as an input image so a ternary image is used as input in its place. The output images (that carry the secret) are binary images. Firstly, image 1 is taken and an error diffusion process is applied to it (giving share 1). Image 2 then has an image hiding error diffusion process applied. During this image hiding error diffusion process, pixels from image 2 are modulated by corresponding pixels of share 1 and the secret image in order to embed the secret into the resultant share of image 2 (giving share 2). The secret is recovered by superimposing share 1 and share 2.

The previously discussed VC schemes all suffer from pixel expansion in that the shares are larger than the original secret image. Chen et al. [41] present a secret sharing scheme that maps a block in a secret image onto a corresponding equal-sized block in the share image without this pixel expansion. Two techniques which are discussed include histogram width-equalization and histogram depth-equalization. This scheme improves the quality of the reconstructed secret when compared with alternative techniques.

Another scheme proposed by Wang et al. [42] uses only Boolean operations. The contrast is also higher than other probabilistic visual cryptography sharing schemes.

The area of contrast within halftone and grayscale VC is an interesting one because the contrast determines exactly how clear the recovered visual secret is. Cimato et al. [43] developed a visual cryptography scheme with ideal contrast by using a technique known as reversing, which was originally discussed by [44]. Reversing changes black pixels to white pixels and vice-versa. Viet and Kurosawa's scheme allows for perfect restoration of the black pixels but only almost perfect restoration of the white pixels. Cimato et al. provide their results for perfect restoration of both black and white pixels. Each share also contained a smaller amount of information than Viet and Kurosawa's which makes it a more desirable and secure scheme. Yang et al. [45] also looked at reversing and the shortcomings of Viet and Kurosawa's scheme. Their work presented a scheme that allowed perfect contrast reconstruction based on any traditional visual cryptography sharing scheme.

4.2 Colour Visual Cryptography

Applying visual cryptography techniques to colour images is a very important area of research because it allows the use of natural colour images to secure some types of information. Due to the nature of a colour image, this again helps to reduce the risk of alerting someone to the fact that information is hidden within it. It should also allow high quality sharing of these colour images. Colour images are also highly popular and have a wider range of uses when compared to other image types. Many of the techniques presented within this section use halftone technologies on the colour images in order to make them work with visual cryptography. That is why colour visual cryptography is presented within this section.

In 1996, Naor and Shamir published a second article on visual cryptography "Visual Cryptography II: Improving the Contrast via the Cover Base" [46]. The new model contains several important changes from their previous work; they use two opaque colours and a completely transparent one.

The first difference is the order in which the transparencies are stacked. There must be an order to correctly recover the secret. Therefore each of the shares needs to be pre-determined and recorded so recovery is possible. The second change is that each participant has c sheets, rather than a single transparency. Each sheet contains red, yellow and transparent pixels. The reconstruction is done by merging the sheets of participant I and participant II, i.e. put the i-th sheet of II on top of the i-th sheet of I and the $(i+1)$-th of I on top of the i-th of II.

The two construction methods are monochromatic construction and bichromatic construction. In the monochromatic construction, each pixel in the original image is mapped into c sub-pixels and each participant holds c sheets. In each of participant I sheets, one of the sub-pixels is red and the remaining $c-1$ sub-pixels are transparent. In each of participant II sheets, one of the sub-pixels is yellow, the other $c-1$ sub-pixels are transparent. The way the sheets of participant I and II are merged is by starting from the sheet number 1 of participant I, then putting sheet number 2 of participant II is put on top of it, then sheet number 2 of participant I on top of that and so on.

The order in which sub-pixels of participant I are coloured red constitutes a permutation π on $\{1, \cdots, c\}$ and the order which the sub-pixels of participant II are coloured yellow constitutes a permutation σ. π and σ are generated as follows: π is chosen uniformly at random from the set of all permutations on c's elements. If the original pixel is yellow, then $\pi = \sigma$, therefore each red sub-pixel of the i-th sheet of participant I will be covered by a yellow sub-pixel of the same position of the i-th sheet of participant II. If the original pixel is red, then $\sigma(i) = \pi(i+1)$ for $1 \leq i \leq c-1$ and $\sigma(c) = \pi(1)$, therefore each yellow sub-pixel of the i-th sheet of participant II will be covered by a red sub-pixel of the same position of the $(i+1)$-th sheet of participant I except the c-th sheet. In practice, the first sheet of participant I is not necessarily stored since it is always covered by other sheets.

Figure 5 shows the results of applying this cover based scheme for a $(2, 2)$-VCS. It is noted that in this example, the original grayscale image is pre-halftoned before it is processed by this scheme.

(a) Original image (200×200) (b) The 1st share S_0 (400×400) (c) The 2nd share S_1 (400×400) (d) The 3rd share S_2 (400×400) (e) The 4th share S_3 (400×400)

(f) The 5th share S_4 (400×400) (g) The 6th share S_5 (400×400) (h) The 7th share S_6 (400×400) (i) The 8th share S_7 (400×400) (j) The stacked image: $S_0, \cdots, S_7$ (400×400)

Fig. 5. Result of a monochromatic construction for $(2, 2)$-VCS using a cover base

A very primitive example of colour image sharing appeared in [47]. In this example, each pixel of the colour secret image is expanded to a block of 2×2 sub-pixels. Each one of these blocks is filled with red, green, blue and white (transparent) colours respectively. Taking symmetries into account, 24 different possibilities for the combination of two pixels can be obtained. It is claimed that if the sub-pixels are small enough, the human visual system will average out the different possible combinations to 24 different colours. To encrypt a pixel of the coloured image, round the colour value of that pixel to the nearest representable colour. Select a random order for the sub-pixels on the first share and select the ordering on the second share such that the combination produces the required colour.

The advantage of this scheme is that it can represent 24 colours with a resolution reduction of 4, instead of $24^2 = 576$. The disadvantage is that the 24 colours are fixed once the basic set of sub-pixel colours is fixed.

An example of a basic $(2, 2)$ colour visual cryptography scheme can be viewed in Figure 6. Two random colour shares are generated. Simply OR'ing each of them allows for the secret to be recovered. The contrast difference is quite noticeable, however the recovered secrets quality is very impressive.

Another primitive scheme was also presented [48] and extended more recently [49]. Verheul and Van Tilborg's scheme provides a c-colour (k, n)-threshold

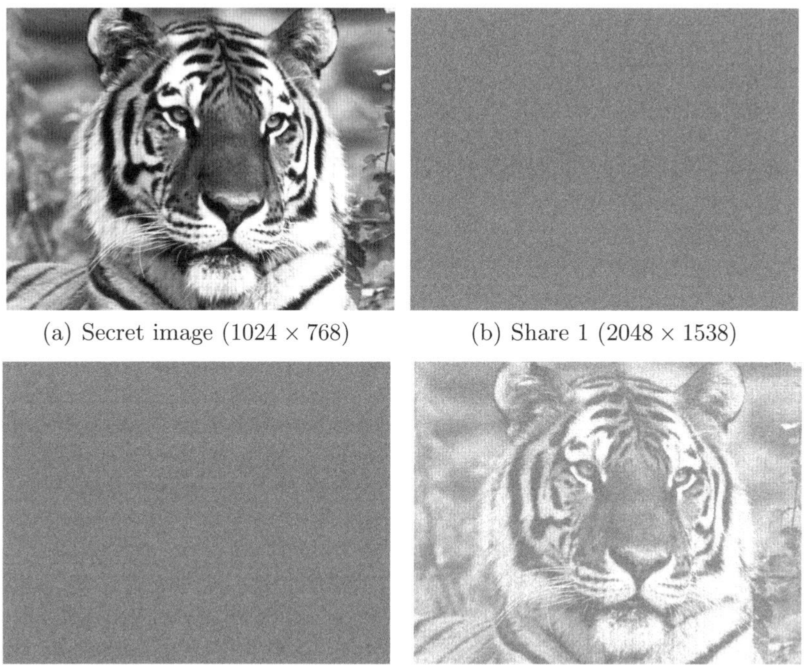

(a) Secret image (1024×768) (b) Share 1 (2048×1538)

(c) Share 2 (2048×1538) (d) Recovered secret (2048×1538)

Fig. 6. Results of a basic colour $(2, 2)$ VC scheme

scheme. This scheme uses the black pixel to superimpose on the result of two colour pixels superimposition, if they give a resultant colour that is not in the original colour palette. This can be achieved by making sure the superimposed colour pixels result in a non-colour palette colour, one of which is changed to a black pixel or by ensuring that one of the colour pixels is changed to black before the superimposing operation [50]. Yang and Laih improve on the pixel expansion aspect of the Verheul and Van Tilborg scheme and their (n, n)-threshold scheme is optimal since they match the following lower bound placed on pixel expansion, formulated in [50]:

$$m \geq \begin{cases} c \cdot 2^{n-1} - 1, & \text{if } n \text{ is even} \\ c \cdot 2^{n-1} - c + 1, & \text{if } n \text{ is odd} \end{cases} \tag{7}$$

Hou et al. [51] proposed a novel approach to share colour images based on halftoning. With this halftone technology, different gray levels can be simulated simply by altering the density of the printed dots. Within bright parts of the image the density is sparse, while in the darker parts of the image, it is dense. This is very helpful in the visual cryptography sense because it is able to transform a grayscale image into a black and white image. This allows for traditional visual cryptography techniques to be applied. Similarly, the colour decomposition method is used for colour images which also allows the proposed scheme to retain all the advantages of traditional visual cryptography, such as no computer participation required for the decryption/recovery of the secret.

Hou himself also provided one of the first colour decomposition techniques to generate visual cryptograms for colour images [52]. Using this colour decomposition, every colour within the image can be decomposed into one of three primary colours: cyan, magenta or yellow. This proposal is similar to traditional visual cryptography with respect to the pixel expansion that occurs. One pixel is expanded into a 2×2 block where two colour pixels are stored along with two transparent (white) pixels.

However, [53] examined the security of Hou's [52] scheme, and while the scheme is secure for a few specific two-colour secret images, the security cannot be guaranteed for many other cases.

An example finite lattice based structure consisting of all 8 colours from the CMYK-RGB colour model has also been proposed [54]. After all the values (each separate colour) have been permuted in each of the 8 lattices, when the 2 shares are generated, the original image will be reproduced when the shares are superimposed.

All the colours within the lattice, $C = \{0, Y, M, C, R, G, B, 1\}$, where 0 represents white and 1 represents black, can be represented within a matrix as follows:

$$\text{White: } \begin{bmatrix} 0 & Y & M & C & 1 & 1 & 1 & 1 \\ 0 & 1 & 1 & 1 & Y & M & C & 1 \end{bmatrix},$$

$$\text{Yellow: } \begin{bmatrix} Y & 0 & M & C & 1 & 1 & 1 & 1 \\ 0 & Y & 1 & 1 & M & C & 1 & 1 \end{bmatrix},$$

$$\text{Magenta:}\quad \begin{bmatrix} M & 0 & C & Y & 1 & 1 & 1 & 1 \\ 0 & M & 1 & 1 & M & C & 1 & 1 \end{bmatrix},$$
$$\text{Cyan:}\quad \begin{bmatrix} C & 0 & Y & M & 1 & 1 & 1 & 1 \\ 0 & C & 1 & 1 & Y & M & 1 & 1 \end{bmatrix},$$
$$\text{Red:}\quad \begin{bmatrix} Y & M & C & 0 & 1 & 1 & 1 & 1 \\ M & Y & 1 & 1 & C & 0 & 1 & 1 \end{bmatrix},$$
$$\text{Green:}\quad \begin{bmatrix} C & Y & M & 0 & 1 & 1 & 1 & 1 \\ Y & C & 1 & 1 & M & 0 & 1 & 1 \end{bmatrix},$$
$$\text{Blue:}\quad \begin{bmatrix} M & C & Y & 0 & 1 & 1 & 1 & 1 \\ C & M & 1 & 1 & Y & 0 & 1 & 1 \end{bmatrix},$$
$$\text{Black:}\quad \begin{bmatrix} Y & M & C & 0 & 1 & 1 & 1 & 1 \\ 1 & 1 & 1 & 1 & Y & M & C & 0 \end{bmatrix},$$

Since, in the above example there are $8 = 4 \times 2$, sub-pixels, the height or width of the image needs to be enlarged by a factor of two before the encryption. Each pixel in the original image is encrypted according to its colour, it is encrypted into an element randomly chosen from one of the lattices. Under such an encryption scheme, the two shares and the reproduced image become $16 = 4 \times 4$ times larger than the original image.

Improving this pixel expansion and also working out the optimal contrast of colour visual cryptography schemes have been investigated [50]. In the paper, they prove that contrast-optimal schemes are available for colour VC and then further go on to prove the optimality with regard to pixel expansion.

A lossless recovery scheme outlined by [55] considers halftoning techniques for the recovery of colour images within visual cryptography. The scheme generates high quality halftone shares which provide lossless recovery of the secrets and reduces the overall noise in the shares without any computational complexity. Their proposed method starts by splitting the colour channels into its constituent parts, cyan (C), magenta (M), and yellow (Y). Each channel has grayscale halftoning applied to it. Error diffusion techniques discussed in [30] are then applied to each halftone channel. A circularly symmetric filter is used along with a Gaussian filter. This provides an adequate structure for the dot placement when constructing the shares.

Lukac and Plataniotis [56] present a scheme based on bit-level operations to provide image encryption for visual cryptography. They argue that the requirements for input restrict the application of VC and the fact that the secret recovery should be done without the use of computation also limits the applicability. Their presented work allows binary, grayscale, and colour images to be used based on their B-bit image sharing scheme. The process takes the input image and breaks it down into its corresponding bit-levels, for example, a grayscale image with 8-bits per pixel is broken down into its corresponding binary bit-levels, from $b = 8$ to $b = 1$ where $b = 1, 2, \cdots, 8$. After the image has been decomposed, traditional VC methods can be applied to each of the binary bit-levels to perform the encryption. An interesting feature of this scheme is that it offers perfect reconstruction of the secret, this is due to its encryption and decryption processes being reciprocal. The performance of this scheme is dependant on the machine, but the results provided in terms of execution time seem acceptable for smaller images. One problem would be the size of the secret to be hidden. The bigger the secret, the longer it will take to encrypt and decrypt. Obviously, this isn't much of a problem with traditional VC methods which cater for instant decryption via stacking the shares. This raises another valid point, the whole idea behind VC is to perform the secret recovery using no computation.

Efficiency within colour visual cryptography [57] is also considered which improves on the work done by [49,58]. The proposed scheme follows Yang and Laih's colour model. The model considers the human visual system's effect on colour combinations out of a set of colour sub-pixels. This means that the set of stacked colour sub-pixels would look like a specific colour in original secret image. As with many other visual cryptography schemes, pixel expansion is an issue. However Shyu's scheme has a pixel expansion of $\lceil log_2 c \rceil$ which is superior to many other colour visual cryptography schemes especially when c, the number of colours in the secret image becomes large. An area for improvement however would be in the examination of the difference between the reconstructed colour pixels and the original secret pixels. Having high quality colour VC shares would further improve on the current schemes examined within this survey, this includes adding a lot of potential for visual authentication and identification.

Chang et al. [59] present a scheme based on smaller shadow images which allows colour image reconstruction when any authorized k shadow images are stacked together using their proposed revealing process. This improves on the following work [60] which presents a scheme that reduces the shadow size by half. Chang et al.'s technique improves on the size of the share in that, as more shares are generated for sharing purposes, the overall size of those shares decreases.

In contrast to colour decomposition, Yang and Chen [61] propose an additive colour mixing scheme based on probabilities. This allows for a fixed pixel expansion and improves on previous colour secret sharing schemes. One problem with this scheme is that the overall contrast is reduced when the secrets are revealed.

In most colour visual cryptography schemes, when the shares are superimposed and the secret is recovered, the colour image gets darker. This is due to the fact that when two pixels of the same colour are superimposed, the resultant pixel gets darker. Cimato et al. [62] examine this colour darkening by proposing a scheme which has to guarantee that the reconstructed secret pixel has the exact same colour as the original. Optimal contrast is also achieved as part of their scheme. This scheme differs from other colour schemes in that it considers only 3 colours when superimposing, black, white, or one pixel of a given colour. This allows for perfect reconstruction of a colour pixel, because no darkening occurs, either by adding a black pixel or by superimposing two colours which are identical, that ultimately results in a final darker colour.

A technique that enables visual cryptography to be used on colour and grayscale images is developed in progressive colour visual cryptography [63]. Many current state of the art visual cryptography techniques lead to the degradation in the quality of the decoded images, which makes it unsuitable for digital media (image, video) sharing and protection. In [63], a series of visual cryptography schemes have been proposed which not only support grayscale and colour images, but also allow high quality images including that of perfect (original) quality to be reconstructed.

The annoying presence of the loss of contrast makes traditional visual cryptography schemes practical only when quality is not an issue which is relatively rare. Therefore, the basic scheme is extended to allow visual cryptography to be directly applied on grayscale and colour images. Image halftoning is employed in order to transform the original image from the grayscale or colour space into the monochrome space which has proved to be quite effective. To further improve the quality, artifacts introduced in the process of halftoning have been reduced by inverse halftoning.

With the use of halftoning and a novel microblock encoding scheme, the technique has a unique flexibility that enables a single encryption of a colour image but enables three types of decryptions on the same ciphertext. The three different types of decryptions enable the recovery of the image of varying qualities. The physical transparency stacking type of decryption enables the recovery of the traditional VC quality image. An enhanced stacking technique enables the decryption into a halftone quality image. A progressive mechanism is established to share colour images at multiple resolutions. Shares are extracted from each resolution layer to construct a hierarchical structure; the images of different resolutions can then be restored by stacking the different shared images together.

The advantage is that this scheme allows for a single encryption, multiple decryptions paradigm. In the scheme, secret images are encrypted / shared once, and later, based on the shares, they can be decrypted / reconstructed in a plurality of ways. Images of different qualities can be extracted, depending on the need for quality as well as the computational resources available. For instance, images with loss of contrast are reconstructed by merely stacking the shares; a simple yet effective bit-wise operation can be applied to restore the halftone image; or images of perfect quality can be restored with the aid of the auxiliary look-up table. Visual cryptography has been extended to allow for multiple resolutions in terms of image quality. Different versions of the original image of different qualities can be reconstructed by selectively merging the shares. Not only this, a spatial multi-resolution scheme has been developed in which images of increasing spatial resolutions can be obtained as more and more shares are employed.

This idea of progressive visual cryptography has recently been extended [64] by generating friendly shares that carry meaningful information and which also allows decryption without any computation at all. Purely stacking the shares reveals the secret. Unlike [63] and [65] which require computation to fully reconstruct the secret, the scheme proposed in [66] has two types of secrets, stacking the transparencies reveals the first, but computation is again required to recover the second-level secret. Fang's scheme is also better than the polynomial sharing method proposed in [67]. The method proposed in [67] is only suitable for digital systems and the computational complexity for encryption and decryption is also a lot higher.

4.3 Quality Evaluation

Grayscale, halftone and colour image techniques for visual cryptography provide an important step for the improvement of VC. The best results are obtained when using error diffusion techniques to spread the pixels as evenly as possible. These results also provide excellent secret recovery because the contrast is high. Using colour images has also improved the potential application for VC, particularly when using computer-specific progressive VC techniques, perfect secret recovery is possible with very high quality colour images and relatively low computational power. However, as discussed, use of computation partially defeats the point of VC.

To measure the quality loss in the meaningful halftone shares, the peak signal-to-noise ratio (PSNR) is used. Firstly the mean squared error must be calculated (Eq. (8)) for all the pixel values in the halftone images. This allows for the PSNR value to be calculated (Eq. (9)).

$$MSE = \frac{1}{nm} \sum_{i=0}^{n-1} \sum_{j=0}^{m-1} \|I(i,j) - K(i,j)\|^2 \tag{8}$$

$$PSNR = 10 \cdot log_{10} \left(\frac{MAX_I^2}{MSE} \right) \tag{9}$$

where I and K are the images with width n and height m. As the share size increases, the visually pleasing attributes improve correspondingly, from an average of 9dB to 12dB, although the overall contrast drops. So a tradeoff must be made in order to obtain good recovered secrets and have suitable quality in the meaningful shares.

5 Multiple Secret Sharing in Visual Cryptography

5.1 Basic Multiple Secret Sharing

The schemes previously discussed deal with sharing just one secret. So the natural extension of that is trying to hide multiple secrets within two shares. Multiple secret sharing has the main advantage of being able to hide more than one secret within a set of shares.

The multiple secret sharing problem was initially examined by Wu and Chen [68]. They concealed two secrets within two sets of shares S_1 and S_2. The first secret is revealed when S_1 and S_2 are superimposed. The second becomes available when S_1 is rotated anti-clockwise 90° and superimposed on S_2. Due to the nature of the angles required for revealing the secrets $(90°, 180°$ or $270°)$ and the fact that this scheme can only share, at most, two secrets, it becomes apparent that it is quite limited in its use.

It is also worth noting that another extended form of secret sharing was proposed [69] that is quite similar to the one discussed which involves stacking the transparencies to reveal a different secret each time a new layer is stacked. An improvement on this extended scheme is achieved by reducing the number of subpixels required [70].

Multiple secret sharing was developed further [71] by designing circular shares so that the limitations of the angle ($\theta = 90°, 180°, 270°$) would no longer be an issue. The secrets can be revealed when S_1 is superimposed on S_2 and rotated clockwise by a certain angle between $0°$ and $360°$.

A further extension of this was implemented [72] which defines another scheme to hide two secret images in two shares with arbitrary rotating angles. This scheme rolls the share images into rings to allow easy rotation of the shares and thus does away with the angle limitation of Wu and Chen's scheme. The recovered secrets are also of better quality when compared to [71], this is due to larger difference between the black and white stacked blocks.

More recently [73] a novel secret sharing scheme was proposed that encodes a set of $x \geq 2$ secrets into two circle shares where x is the number of secrets to be shared. This is one of the first set of results presented that is capable of sharing more than two secrets using traditional visual cryptography methods. The algorithms presented can also be extended to work with grayscale images by using halftone techniques. Colour images could also be employed by using colour decomposition [52] or colour composition [57].

One difficulty with this scheme is the pixel expansion. The expansion is twice the number of secrets to be hidden, so the size of the circle shares increases dramatically when many large secrets are hidden. However, the number of secrets that are contained within the shares still remains a secret unless supplementary lines are added to the circle shares to ease the alignment. This is another problem with sharing multiple secrets, especially when dealing with circle shares, knowing the correct alignment points. Knowing how many secrets are actually contained within the shares is also a concern. If the rotation angle is small (meaning many secrets are concealed) and rotation of the shares occurs too quickly, it is possible that all secrets may not be recovered.

Sharing a set of secrets where that set contains more than 2 secrets, using traditional visual cryptography and typical polygonal shapes has also been considered [74]. This scheme presents three joint VC methods for sharing secrets. The first deals with altering the contrast of the shares, which allows multiple secrets to be hidden within a set of shares. This scheme keeps the original aspect ratio of the secrets, but results in darker shares after superimposing has taken place. The revealing share (key share) is also of a smaller size than the share which contains each of the secrets. The second scheme presents a way of using the even and odd scan lines of a share to embed two secrets. This helps with the overall contrast of the white areas of the shares, but also reduces the overall contrast of the recovered secrets. The aspect ratio has also been altered. Finally the multiple joint combination of shares results in two shares which share four secrets. While the aspect ratio remains intact, the overall contrast drops

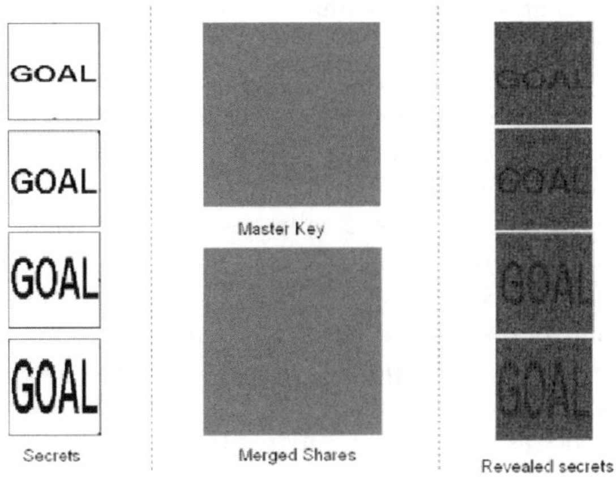

Fig. 7. Joint visual cryptography with multiple secrets, their corresponding shares and the recovered secrets

significantly when more secrets are added. This becomes a problem if many secrets are to be considered. Figure 7 shows this scheme sharing four secrets, the word "GOAL" increases in size as the master key share is moved around.

Another new scheme [75] considers secret sharing for multiple secrets, which is established on a stacking based graph approach to reconstructing the pixels. By stacking the shares at aliquot angles, the secrets can be revealed. Feng et al.'s proposed scheme is formally defined as a 2-out-of-2 m-way extended visual cryptography secret sharing scheme for m secret images, denoted as: $(2, 2)$-m-VSSM. As with many other visual cryptography schemes, this scheme also allows for decryption without the use of computation. Once the shares are positioned at their aliquot angles, the secrets are instantly revealed.

The creation (encryption) of the shares works as follows. Firstly a relationship graph is created between the rows, this is because each row in the scheme is considered independently. For each row, the blocks are collected in the position of the two share images at the required angles $0, \frac{360^\circ}{m}, \frac{360^\circ}{m} \times 2, \cdots, \frac{360^\circ}{m} \times (m-1)$ to form the graph. Every block is related to all the share blocks in the other share image. Therefore, all the share blocks on a row can be separated into sets. These blocks and sets are then combined with the visual patterns developed by Feng et al. [75] and the shares are generated.

Yet another problem with this scheme is the pixel expansion $2m$, where m is the number of secrets to be shared. Again the overall size of the shares increases drastically when more secrets are considered. The contrast of the scheme is also a problem. The previously discussed schemes originated from Wu and Chen, Hsu et al. provide better contrast whereas Feng et al.'s contrast is $\frac{1}{3m}$. This means the more secrets added, the lower the contrast gets, so overall image quality deteriorates.

Multiple secret sharing using weighted transparencies is discussed here [76]. Based on an extended style of visual cryptography, stacking qualified subsets of transparencies reveals a different secret at each stacking level. The transparencies with the largest weight determine which images are recovered. The typically advantageous properties of VC are used within this scheme along with a max-weight dominance and a quality-control design to create high quality shares.

Traditional visual cryptography usually leads to inefficiency when shares are electronically stored and transferred. Gnanaguruparan and Kak [77] proposed a way of hiding multiple secret images in one pair of shares thus to improve the efficiency. One share of the large secret image is constructed from the joint shares of the small secret image. This process repeats for even smaller secret images. This recursive hiding scheme utilizes shares in a more efficient way and the efficiency is almost twice as high when compared to traditional visual cryptography schemes.

The efficiency of sharing multiple secrets against sharing a single secret has also been looked at [78]. Checking to see if improvements are even possible are examined along with a proposed scheme that helps to achieve these improvements. A bound is proved to highlight these improvements.

5.2 Colour Multiple Secret Sharing

Using halftone and colour images as a base or cover for multiple secret sharing is an interesting topic. Techniques proposed within [79] allow for a smaller set of shares (which can be unique) to be hidden with these meaningful colour images. Using the idea of a master key is capable of recovering all the secrets which have been generated using the outlined scheme, it is used to cover the halftone or colour image in order to reveal the secrets. The secret shares in this case are embedded within the cover images, this helps to remove suspicion that any encryption has taken place or, that the image has even been altered in any specific noticeable way. Figure 8 illustrates the application of this scheme.

(a) The original colour image containing the merged share.
(b) Secure mask to superimpose.
(c) Secrets revealed after superimposing (b) on (a).

Fig. 8. Merging a share of visual cryptography with a colour image

5.3 Quality Evaluation

Sharing multiple secrets with high quality recovery is very achievable. Depending on the number of secrets a user wishes to hide, this determines the overall size of the shares. The more secrets a user wishes to hide, the larger the resultant shares get. This is one of the shortcomings of multiple secret sharing, the final share size when many large secrets are considered can become unmanageable. Numerous schemes are presented which range from sharing just two secrets to the general case of sharing any number of secrets. Of the schemes presented, circular shares seem to be best in terms of the secrets recovery and contrast. The scheme presented for sharing more than two secrets using standard rectangular shares has issues with contrast while more secrets are added. Using a colour cover image also presents an effective way to share multiple smaller secrets. The difference between the original and the merged shares is not very noticeable to the visual system.

An objective way of testing the actual alteration between the original Lenna image and the Lenna image which contains the merged share is to use the peak signal-to-noise ratio (PSNR) metric to measure this difference.

The PSNR for an $n \times m$ colour image I and its noisy counterpart K is calculated thusly, first, the mean squared error (MSE) must be calculated on each pixel for each of its corresponding RGB channels using Eq. (8). After which, each channel's PSNR value, must be calculated using Eq. (9). The values are then summed and averaged, resulting in the final PSNR value. MAX is the maximum pixel value, 255 in a colour image.

The PSNR between the original image and the image in Figure 8(a) is 21.0715dB, which is an acceptable value of quality loss considering the images secure properties.

Overall, the majority of the multiple secret sharing schemes are successful in effectively hiding two or more secrets with a set of shares. The schemes that roll the secrets into circular shares prove to be the most interesting and effective in terms of sharing many secrets with very high contrast.

6 Visual Cryptography Applications

6.1 Watermarking

Practical uses for visual cryptography come in the form of watermarking. Memon and Wong [80] propose various techniques by which these watermarks can be applied to images. A simple watermark insertion scheme is illustrated [81]. However it is not robust because the watermark is embedded within the least significant bit of the image and could easily be destroyed. A more robust scheme should be able to deal with lossy image compression, filtering, and scanning. The idea of random noise [82] is employed on colour images to make removal of the watermark very difficult. Cryptographic functions such as the MD5 hash [83] have also been employed to improve the security features when it comes to embedding data within images. Similarly [84] also explores the use of watermarks within visual cryptography.

A digital image copyright scheme based on visual cryptography is presented within [85]. It is simple and efficient, both in watermark embedding and retrieval. It is also acceptably robust when the watermarked image is compressed. After compression, the watermark can still be recovered and verified. However, the scheme is not robust in terms of minor modifications to the watermarked image. Accurate recovery is not possible. Another problem is that the watermark could be successfully recovered from an image exhibiting some similarities with the original, even though the image is not the original.

Rather than the random pixel selection scheme proposed within [85] [86] provides a scheme by which specific pixels from the original image are selected. One issue with this non-random scheme is that any changes made on the original, such as defacement of the image, will be reflected in the restored watermark. The watermark is still recognizable but distortions are noticeable. An important part of this scheme, however, is that the watermark itself is invisible. This means that the original image looks exactly the same as the watermarked image. The scheme is robust to minor changes in the image, but those changes are present in the recovered watermark. The key used to recover the watermark depends on the security of the scheme. If a small key is used (8-bits), the scheme will not be as secure as a key of length 128-bits. The watermark also remains hidden until the key is employed to recover it.

A further improvement on Hwang's scheme [85] comes in the form of another VC based watermarking scheme [87]. This improved scheme supports black and white images as well as colour images and is robust against scaling and rotation of the watermarked image. Robust recovery of the watermark is also possible after the image has been defaced. As with the other schemes previously discussed, this scheme is also key dependant. Without the key, no watermark recovery is possible.

One of the most robust ways to hide a secret within natural images is by typically employing visual cryptography based on halftone techniques. The perfect scheme is extremely practical and can reveal secrets without computer participation. Recent state of the art watermarking [88] can hide a watermark in documents which require no specific key in order to retrieve it. Removing the need for a key is quite important because it further increases the security and robustness of the watermarking process.

Hou and Chen [89] implemented an asymmetric watermarking scheme based on visual cryptography. Two shares are generated to hold the watermark. One is embedded into the cover-image and another is kept as a secret key for the watermark extraction. The watermark is extracted using traditional stacking properties of visual cryptography. The watermark is robust in that it is difficult to change or remove and can withstand a number of attacks.

6.2 Moiré Patterns

A potential application for visual cryptography is its use in conjunction with Moiré patterns. Moiré patterns [90] (or fringes) are induced when a revealing layer such as a dot screen or line grating is superimposed on top of a periodically repeating shape. The resulting Moiré pattern is influenced by changing any of the following geometric parameters characterizing the individual grid structures, namely period, orientation, and shape [91,92,93]. Whether a dot screen or a line grating is used, both induce Moiré fringes with the same geometric properties [94].

The revealing layer contains horizontal black lines (line grating), between those lines is transparent white space. When the revealing layer is superimposed, the shapes that appear are the magnified versions of the repeating pattern. This magnifying property [95,96] could be used as a method of locating hidden VC shares within a Moiré pattern.

This magnification factor of these patterns can be calculated as follows, let p_b represent the period of shapes in the base layer, the period of the line gratings in the revealing layer is denoted as p_r. In order for the magnification to work, the periods must be sufficiently close. When the revealing layer is superimposed, the repeating pattern in the base layer is stretched along the vertical axis. There is no change in the horizontal axis. This magnification can be represented as p_m [97]. The following equation expresses this magnification along the vertical axis:

$$p_m = -\frac{p_b \cdot p_r}{p_b - p_r} \tag{10}$$

If p_m is negative, this represents a mirrored magnified shape along the vertical axis.

Visual cryptography has been implemented using Moiré patterns. Desmedt and Le [98] provide a scheme by which secrecy and anonymity are both satisfied. Moiré patterns occur when high frequency lattices are combined together to produce low frequency lattice patterns. It is the difference in these high frequencies that give the Moiré patterns. Figure 9 shows an example of these Moiré patterns.

The Moiré cryptography model is as follows: The embedded (secret) image is randomized into two shares, known as pre-shares. Each of these are independent of the original image. XORing these pre-shares will recover the original. Next,

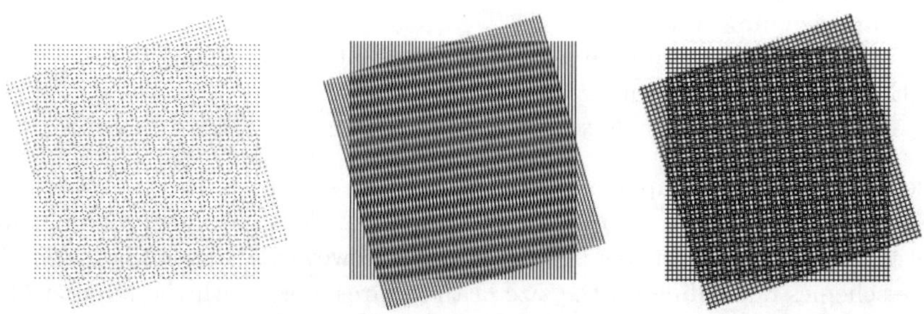

(a) Superimposing two dot screens (b) Superimposing two line gratings (c) Superimposing two grids

Fig. 9. Moiré patterns generated with different styles

the hiding algorithm takes the cover image and combines it with each of the pre-shares separately. Its output is the final two shares that are used to reveal the original embedded image. These resulting shares look the same as the input cover image that is used.

There are three different Moiré schemes proposed by Desmedt and Le [98], lattice rotation, lattice smooth rotation, and dot orientation. The problem with lattice rotation is that the boundary between differently-rotated areas in the shares becomes visible. However, this scheme produced very sharp decrypted ciphertext. Lattice smooth rotation fixed the boundary issues but introduced another problem, namely, the artifacts introduced into the shares stand out too much and become visible. The pair settled on the final scheme, dot orientation, as their chosen implementation. The dots from the shares are converted into diamond shape "dots", this makes for a less visible boundary than circular or elliptical dots. The scheme encodes a white pixel by superimposing two squares onto the shares whose dots are oriented at different angles. To encode a black pixel, dot patterns are used that are of the same angle. This produces two different Moiré patterns for the white and black dots. That means this scheme uses the Moiré patterns to recover the secret embedded image, rather than traditional visual cryptography schemes which use the gray level of the squares to recover the secret.

These Moiré patterns could be used in conjunction with hologram technology [99]. This could provide secure solutions for verification of generated holograms.

7 Conclusion and Future Work

7.1 Conclusion

It is apparent that a lot of time and effort have been dedicated to visual secret sharing using visual cryptography. Many of the schemes presented work extremely well and the current state of the art techniques have proven to be very useful for many applications, such as verification and authentication.

The following trends have been identified within visual cryptography:

1. Contrast improvement.
2. Share size improvement.
3. Wider range of suitable image types (binary to colour images).
4. Efficiency of VC schemes.
5. Ability to share multiple secrets.

Essentially the most important part of any VC scheme is the contrast of the recovered secret from a particular set of shares. Ideal schemes provide a high contrast when the secret has been recovered. However, a tradeoff is required in some schemes depending on the size of the shares along with the number of secrets which may be concealed. Especially within extended visual cryptography schemes, contrast is of major importance. Making sure the base images completely disappear and a clear secret is recovered which could be another high quality image is vitally important.

Some schemes present methods which do not work with printed transparencies and these rely on computation in order to recover the secret. In this respect, high quality secret recovery is possible, however it is preferred if the scheme works with printed transparencies. After all, this is the idea behind VC. Conversely, if an application requires digital recovery of the secrets, then perfect recovery can be achieved via the XOR operation.

Improving on the resultant share size has also been a worthwhile research topic. Having shares that are close to the original secret's size is best, because it results in shares that are easier to manage and transmit. Large secrets with even larger shares become cumbersome. However, at times a tradeoff must be made between the size of the shares and the contrast of the recovered secret. The tradeoff between size and the secret recovery must be suitable so that high quality recovery can take place and must also ensure that the shares do not expand into large, unmanageable sizes.

The use of grayscale and colour images has added value to the field of visual cryptography. Reducing the requirements on input image type so that any kind of image can be used to share a secret is very important. The fact that any image can be used to share a secret within visual cryptography shows a great improvement on the very initial work that required an image to be converted to its binary equivalent before any processing could be done on it. However, the application of the scheme depends greatly on the type of images to be input.

Efficiency covers a number of things which have already been discussed, such as contrast and share size. The topic of efficiency also includes how the shares and images have been processed. Numerous methods presented within this survey have improved on prior work and techniques, resulting in schemes that are highly efficient and very simple to implement and use. For the maximum efficiency in recovering the secret, no computer participation should be involved.

The addition of multiple secret sharing has proven to be an interesting area within VC. This further increases the capacity of VC as it allows the same physical amount of data to be sent, ie. two shares, but increases the amount of usable information retrievable at the end.

Overall, this survey has summarized much of the work done in the area of visual cryptography and has also provided a number of ideas for new research within this domain. There are still many topics worth exploring within VC to further expand on its potential in terms of secret sharing, data security, identification, and authentication.

7.2 Future Work

The previously mentioned trends that have emerged within VC require more attention. This allows VC to remain an important research topic. Typically within multiple secret sharing, the alignment points can cause problems. A novel multiple secret sharing scheme that does away with the need for supplementary lines could possibly be grounds for new research.

Future work that would further the progress of visual cryptography would be to examine and create suitable schemes for other image types, such as hatched or line-art based images [100]. The focus being, to apply these techniques in conjunction with modern day image hatching techniques which would allow the extension of VC into the currency domain, potentially making it applicable to a wider range of secure applications, such as within the banking industry.

The use of these types of shares within the secure printing industry should also be considered. For example, creating shares that can be printed using normal print techniques, but when scanned or photocopied, react in an adverse way. This would prevent unauthorized copying of the shares.

Extending the print and scan application of VC [101] may also be considered. Print and scan protection is one possible avenue of research, which would render the shares useless after scanning has taken place. Scanning a share into a computer system and then digitally superimposing its corresponding share could also be considered. This may well prove to be very challenging due to the nature of the scanned shares not being an exact copy and having to work out the borders of the scanned image. Rotation of the resultant scan would also have to be taken into consideration. This would have the potential for secure verification of tickets or other forms of document verification, such as secure barcode scanning.

References

1. Shamir, A.: How to share a secret. Communications of the ACM 22(11), 612–613 (1979)
2. Naor, M., Shamir, A.: Visual cryptography. In: De Santis, A. (ed.) EUROCRYPT 1994. LNCS, vol. 950, pp. 1–12. Springer, Heidelberg (1994)
3. Blundo, C., D'Arco, P., De Santis, A., Stinson, D.R.: Contrast optimal threshold visual cryptography schemes. SIAM Journal on Discrete Mathematics 16(2), 224–261 (2003)
4. Lau, D.L., Arce, G.R.: Modern Digital Halftoning. Marcel Dekker, New York (2000)
5. Ateniese, G., Blundo, C., De Santis, A., Stinson, D.R.: Extended schemes for visual cryptography. Theoretical Computer Science 250, 1–16 (1996)
6. Ateniese, G., Blundo, C., De Santis, A., Stinson, D.R.: Visual cryptography for general access structures. Information and Computation 129(2), 86–106 (1996)
7. Yang, C.N., Chen, T.S.: Extended visual secret sharing schemes with high-quality shadow images using gray sub pixels. In: Kamel, M.S., Campilho, A.C. (eds.) ICIAR 2005. LNCS, vol. 3656, pp. 1184–1191. Springer, Heidelberg (2005)
8. Ito, R., Kuwakado, H., Tanaka, H.: Image size invariant visual cryptography. IEICE Transactions E82-A(10), 2172–2177 (1999)
9. Tzeng, W.G., Hu, C.M.: A new approach for visual cryptography. Designs, Codes and Cryptography 27(3), 207–227 (2002)
10. Yang, C.N.: New visual secret sharing schemes using probabilistic method. Pattern Recognition Letters 25(4), 481–494 (2004)
11. Yang, C.N., Chen, T.S.: New size-reduced visual secret sharing schemes with half reduction of shadow size. IEICE Transactions 89-A(2), 620–625 (2006)

12. Yang, C.N., Chen, T.S.: Visual secret sharing scheme: Improving the contrast of a recovered image via different pixel expansions. In: Campilho, A., Kamel, M.S. (eds.) ICIAR 2006. LNCS, vol. 4141, pp. 468–479. Springer, Heidelberg (2006)
13. Yang, C.N., Chen, T.S.: Aspect ratio invariant visual secret sharing schemes with minimum pixel expansion. Pattern Recognition Letters 26(2), 193–206 (2005)
14. Yang, C.N., Chen, T.S.: Size-adjustable visual secret sharing schemes. IEICE Transactions 88-A(9), 2471–2474 (2005)
15. Yang, C.N., Chen, T.S.: Reduce shadow size in aspect ratio invariant visual secret sharing schemes using a square block-wise operation. Pattern Recognition 39(7), 1300–1314 (2006)
16. Kim, C.H., Seong, S.M., Lee, J.A., Kim, L.S.: Winscale: an image-scaling algorithm using an area pixel model. IEEE Transactions on Circuits and Systems for Video Technology 13(6), 549–553 (2003)
17. Gonzalez, R.C., Woods, R.E.: Digital Image Processing. Addison-Wesley Longman Publishing Co., Inc., Boston (2001)
18. Hofmeister, T., Krause, M., Simon, H.U.: Contrast-optimal k out of n secret sharing schemes in visual cryptography. Theoretical Computer Science 240(2), 471–485 (2000)
19. Tuyls, P., Hollmann, H.D.L., van Lint, J.H., Tolhuizen, L.M.G.M.: XOR-based visual cryptography schemes. Designs, Codes and Cryptography 37(1), 169–186 (2005)
20. Yang, C.N., Chen, T.S.: An image secret sharing scheme with the capability of previvewing the secret image. In: ICME 2007, pp. 1535–1538 (2007)
21. Thien, C.C., Lin, J.C.: Secret image sharing. Computers & Graphics 26, 765–770 (2002)
22. Wang, R.Z., Su, C.H.: Secret image sharing with smaller shadow images. Pattern Recognition Letters 27(6), 551–555 (2006)
23. Horng, G., Chen, T., Tsai, D.S.: Cheating in visual cryptography. Des. Codes Cryptography 38(2), 219–236 (2006)
24. Naor, M., Pinkas, B.: Visual authentication and identification. In: Kaliski Jr., B.S. (ed.) CRYPTO 1997. LNCS, vol. 1294, pp. 322–336. Springer, Heidelberg (1997)
25. Yang, C., Laih, C.: Some new types of visual secret sharing schemes, vol. III, pp. 260–268 (December 1999)
26. Hu, C.M., Tzeng, W.G.: Cheating prevention in visual cryptography. IEEE Transactions on Image Processing 16(1), 36–45 (2007)
27. Biehl, I., Wetzel, S.: Traceable visual cryptography. In: Han, Y., Quing, S. (eds.) ICICS 1997. LNCS, vol. 1334, pp. 61–71. Springer, Heidelberg (1997)
28. Kang, H.R.: Digital Color Halftoning. In: Society of Photo-Optical Instrumentation Engineers (SPIE), Bellingham, WA, USA (1999)
29. Campbell, A.: The Designer's Lexicon. Chronicle Books, San Francisco (2000)
30. Zhou, Z., Arce, G.R., Crescenzo, G.D.: Halftone visual cryptography. IEEE Transactions on Image Processing 15(8), 2441–2453 (2006)
31. Myodo, E., Sakazawa, S., Takishima, Y.: Visual cryptography based on void-and-cluster halftoning technique. In: ICIP, pp. 97–100 (2006)
32. Myodo, E., Takagi, K., Miyaji, S., Takishima, Y.: Halftone visual cryptography embedding a natural grayscale image based on error diffusion technique. In: ICME, pp. 2114–2117 (2007)
33. Wang, Z., Arce, G.R.: Halftone visual cryptography through error diffusion. In: ICIP, pp. 109–112 (2006)
34. Ateniese, G., Blundo, C., De Santis, A., Stinson, D.R.: Extended capabilities for visual cryptography. Theoretical Computer Science 250(1-2), 143–161 (2001)

35. Nakajima, M., Yamaguchi, Y.: Extended visual cryptography for natural images. In: WSCG, pp. 303–310 (2002)
36. Zhang, Y.: Space-filling curve ordered dither. Computers & Graphics 22(4), 559–563 (1998)
37. Lin, C.C., Tsai, W.H.: Visual cryptography for gray-level images by dithering techniques. Pattern Recognition Letters 24(1-3), 349–358 (2003)
38. Fu, M.S., Au, O.C.: A novel method to embed watermark in different halftone images: data hiding by conjugate error diffusion (dhced). In: ICME 2003, Washington, DC, USA, pp. 609–612. IEEE Computer Society, Los Alamitos (2003)
39. Wu, C.W., Thompson, G.R., Stanich, M.J.: Digital watermarking and steganography via overlays of halftone images. In: SPIE, vol. 5561, pp. 152–163 (2004)
40. Ulichney, R.A.: Digital Halftoning. MIT Press, Cambridge (1987)
41. Chen, Y.F., Chan, Y.K., Huang, C.C., Tsai, M.H., Chu, Y.P.: A multiple-level visual secret-sharing scheme without image size expansion. Information Sciences 177(21), 4696–4710 (2007)
42. Wang, D., Zhang, L., Ma, N., Li, X.: Two secret sharing schemes based on boolean operations. Pattern Recognition 40(10), 2776–2785 (2007)
43. Cimato, S., De Santis, A., Ferrara, A.L., Masucci, B.: Ideal contrast visual cryptography schemes with reversing. Information Processing Letters 93(4), 199–206 (2005)
44. Duong, Q.V., Kurosawa, K.: Almost ideal contrast visual cryptography with reversing. In: Okamoto, T. (ed.) CT-RSA 2004. LNCS, vol. 2964, pp. 353–365. Springer, Heidelberg (2004)
45. Yang, C.N., Wang, C.C., Chen, T.S.: Real perfect contrast visual secret sharing schemes with reversing. In: Zhou, J., Yung, M., Bao, F. (eds.) ACNS 2006. LNCS, vol. 3989, pp. 433–447. Springer, Heidelberg (2006)
46. Naor, M., Shamir, A.: Visual cryptography ii: Improving the contrast via the cover base. In: Lomas, M. (ed.) Security Protocols 1996. LNCS, vol. 1189, pp. 197–202. Springer, Heidelberg (1997)
47. Rijmen, V., Preneel, B.: Efficient color visual encryption for shared colors of benetton. In: EUCRYPTO 1996 (1996)
48. Verheul, E.R., Tilborg, H.C.A.V.: Constructions and properties of k out of n visual secret sharing schemes. Des. Codes Cryptography 11(2), 179–196 (1997)
49. Yang, C.N., Laih, C.S.: New colored visual secret sharing schemes. Designs, Codes and Cryptography 20(3), 325–336 (2000)
50. Cimato, S., De Prisco, R., De Santis, A.: Optimal colored threshold visual cryptography schemes. Designs, Codes and Cryptography 35(3), 311–335 (2005)
51. Hou, Y.C., Chang, C.Y., Tu, S.F.: Visual cryptography for color images based on halftone technology. Image, Acoustic, Speech and Signal Processing, Part 2 (2001)
52. Hou, Y.C.: Visual cryptography for color images. Pattern Recognition 36, 1619–1629 (2003)
53. Leung, B.W., Ng, F.Y., Wong, D.S.: On the security of a visual cryptography scheme for color images. Pattern Recognition (August 2008)
54. Koga, H., Yamamoto, H.: Proposal of a lattice-based visual secret sharing scheme for color and grey-scale images. IEICE Transactions Fundamentals E81-A(6), 1262–1269 (1998)
55. Krishna Prakash, N., Govindaraju, S.: Visual secret sharing schemes for color images using halftoning. Proceedings of Computational Intelligence and Multimedia Applications 3, 174–178 (2007)

56. Lukac, R., Plataniotis, K.N.: Bit-level based secret sharing for image encryption. Pattern Recognition 38(5), 767–772 (2005)
57. Shyu, S.J.: Efficient visual secret sharing scheme for color images. Pattern Recognition 39(5), 866–880 (2006)
58. Blundo, C., De Bonis, A., De Santis, A.: Improved schemes for visual cryptography. Designs, Codes and Cryptography 24(3), 255–278 (2001)
59. Chang, C.C., Lin, C.C., Lin, C.H., Chen, Y.H.: A novel secret image sharing scheme in color images using small shadow images. Information Sciences 178(11), 2433–2447 (2008)
60. Yang, C.N., Chen, T.S.: New size-reduced visual secret sharing schemes with half reduction of shadow size. In: Gervasi, O., Gavrilova, M.L., Kumar, V., Laganá, A., Lee, H.P., Mun, Y., Taniar, D., Tan, C.J.K. (eds.) ICCSA 2005. LNCS, vol. 3480, pp. 19–28. Springer, Heidelberg (2005)
61. Yang, C.N., Chen, T.S.: Colored visual cryptography scheme based on additive color mixing. Pattern Recognition 41(10), 3114–3129 (2008)
62. Cimato, S., De Prisco, R., De Santis, A.: Colored visual cryptography without color darkening. Theoretical Computer Science 374(1-3), 261–276 (2007)
63. Jin, D., Yan, W.Q., Kankanhalli, M.S.: Progressive color visual cryptography. SPIE Journal of Electronic Imaging 14(3) (2005)
64. Fang, W.P.: Friendly progressive visual secret sharing. Pattern Recognition 41(4), 1410–1414 (2008)
65. Chen, S.K., Lin, J.C.: Fault-tolerant and progressive transmission of images. Pattern Recognition 38(12), 2466–2471 (2005)
66. Fang, W.P., Lin, J.C.: Visual cryptography with extra ability of hiding confidential data. Journal of Electronic Imaging 15(2), 023020 (2006)
67. Thien, C.C., Lin, J.C.: An image-sharing method with user-friendly shadow images. IEEE Transactions on Circuits and Systems for Video Technology 13(12), 1161–1169 (2003)
68. Wu, C., Chen, L.: A study on visual cryptography. Master's thesis, Institute of Computer and Information Science, National Chiao Tung University, Taiwan, R.O.C. (1998)
69. Katoh, T., Imai, H.: An extended construction method for visual secret sharing schemes. IEICE Transactions J79-A(8), 1344–1351 (1996)
70. Yang, C.N., Chen, T.S.: Extended visual secret sharing schemes: Improving the shadow image quality. IJPRAI 21(5), 879–898 (2007)
71. Wu, H.C., Chang, C.C.: Sharing visual multi-secrets using circle shares. Computer Standards & Interfaces 28, 123–135 (2005)
72. Hsu, H.C., Chen, T.S., Lin, Y.H.: The ringed shadow image technology of visual cryptography by applying diverse rotating angles to hide the secret sharing. Networking, Sensing and Control 2, 996–1001 (2004)
73. Shyu, S.J., Huang, S.Y., Lee, Y.K., Wang, R.Z., Chen, K.: Sharing multiple secrets in visual cryptography. Pattern Recognition 40(12), 3633–3651 (2007)
74. Weir, J., Yan, W.Q.: Sharing multiple secrets using visual cryptography. In: IEEE ISCAS 2009, Taiwan (2009)
75. Feng, J.B., Wu, H.C., Tsai, C.S., Chang, Y.F., Chu, Y.P.: Visual secret sharing for multiple secrets. Pattern Recognition 41(12), 3572–3581 (2008)
76. Chen, S.K.: A visual cryptography based system for sharing multiple secret images. In: ISCGAV 2007: Proceedings of the 7th WSEAS International Conference on Signal Processing, Computational Geometry & Artificial Vision, Stevens Point, Wisconsin, USA, World Scientific and Engineering Academy and Society (WSEAS), pp. 117–122 (2007)

77. Gnanaguruparan, M., Kak, S.: Recursive hiding of secrets in visual cryptography. Cryptologia 26(1), 68–76 (2002)
78. Crescenzo, G.D.: Sharing one secret vs. sharing many secrets. Theoretical Computer Science 295(1-3), 123–140 (2003)
79. Weir, J., Yan, W., Crookes, D.: Secure mask for color image hidding. In: Communications and Networking in China, ChinaCom 2008, August 2008, pp. 1304–1307 (2008)
80. Memon, N., Wong, P.W.: Protecting digital media content. Communications of the ACM 41(7), 35–43 (1998)
81. van Schyndel, R.G., Tirkel, A.Z., Osborne, C.F.: A digital watermark. In: ICIP(2), pp. 86–90 (1994)
82. Braudaway, G.W., Magerlein, K.A., Mintzer, F.: Protecting publicly available images with a visible image watermark. In: van Renesse, R.L. (ed.) Society of Photo-Optical Instrumentation Engineers (SPIE) Conference Series, March 1996. Society of Photo-Optical Instrumentation Engineers (SPIE) Conference Series, vol. 2659, pp. 126–133 (1996)
83. Wong, P.W.: A watermark for image integrity and ownership verification. In: PICS, IS&T - The Society for Imaging Science and Technology, pp. 374–379 (1998)
84. Luo, H., Pan, J.S., Lu, Z.M.: Hiding multiple watermarks in transparencies of visual cryptography. Intelligent Information Hiding and Multimedia Signal Processing 1, 303–306 (2007)
85. Hwang, R.J.: A digital image copyright protection scheme based on visual cryptography. Tamkang Journal of Science and Engineering 3(2), 97–106 (2000)
86. Hassan, M.A., Khalili, M.A.: Self watermarking based on visual cryptography. Proceedings of World Academy of Science, Engineering and Technology 8, 159–162 (2005)
87. Sleit, A., Abusitta, A.: A visual cryptography based watermark technology for individual and group images. Systemics, Cybernetics And Informatics 5(2), 24–32
88. Chuang, S.C., Huang, C.H., Wu, J.L.: Unseen visible watermarking. In: ICIP(3), pp. 261–264. IEEE, Los Alamitos (2007)
89. Hou, Y.C., Chen, P.M.: An asymmetric watermarking scheme based on visual cryptography. In: WCCC-ICSP 5th International Conference on Signal Processing Proceedings, vol. 2, pp. 992–995 (2000)
90. Hersch, R.D., Chosson, S.: Band moiré images. In: ACM SIGGRAPH 2004, pp. 239–247. ACM, New York (2004)
91. Knotts, M.E., Hemphill, R.G.: Selected papers on optical moiré and applications. Optics & Photonics News, 53–55 (August 1996)
92. Kafri, O., Glatt, I.: The physics of Moire metrology. Wiley, New York (1990)
93. Indebetouw, G., Czarnek, R.: Selected papers on optical moiré and applications. SPIE Milestones Series, vol. MS64 (1992)
94. Amidror, I.: The Theory of the Moiré Phenomenon. Kluwer, Dordrecht (2000)
95. Hutley, M., Stevens, R.: Optical inspection of arrays and periodic structures using moire magnification. In: Searching for Information: Artificial Intelligence and Information Retrieval Approaches (Ref. No. 1999/199), IEE Two-day Seminar, pp. 8/1–8/5 (1999)
96. Kamal, H., Völkel, R., Alda, J.: Properties of moir[e-acute] magnifiers. Optical Engineering 37(11), 3007–3014 (1998)

97. Gabrielyan, E.: Shape moiré patterns (March 2007), http://switzernet.com/people/emin-gabrielyan/070320-shape-moire/
98. Desmedt, Y., Le, T.V.: Moiré cryptography. In: ACM Conference on Computer and Communications Security, pp. 116–124 (2000)
99. Liu, S., Zhang, X., Lai, H.: Artistic effect and application of moireé patterns in security holograms. Applied Optics 34(22), 4700–4702 (1995)
100. Praun, E., Hoppe, H., Webb, M., Finkelstein, A.: Real-time hatching. In: ACM SIGGRAPH 2001, pp. 579–584. ACM, New York (2001)
101. Yan, W.Q., Jin, D., Kankanhalli, M.S.: Visual cryptography for print and scan applications. In: Proceedings of International Symposium on Circuits and Systems, Vancouver, Canada, May 2004, pp. 572–575 (2004)

Secure Masks for Visual Cryptography

Jonathan Weir and WeiQi Yan

Queen's University Belfast, Belfast, BT7 1NN, UK

Abstract. Visual cryptography provides a very powerful technique by which one secret can be distributed into two or more pieces known as shares. When the shares are printed on transparencies and then superimposed exactly together, the original secret can be recovered without computer participation. In this paper, we take multiple secrets into consideration and generate a key share for all the secrets; correspondingly, we share each secret using this key share. The secrets are recovered when the key is superimposed on the combined share in different locations using the proposed scheme. Also discussed and illustrated within this paper is how to embed a share of visual cryptography into halftone and colour images. The remaining share is used as a key share in order to perform the decryption. It is also worth noting that no information regarding the secrets is leaked in any of our proposed schemes. We provide the corresponding results in this paper.

1 Introduction

Visual cryptography was originally invented and pioneered by Naor and Shamir [1]. Visual cryptography is a cryptographic scheme, which can decode concealed images without any cryptographic computation. As the name, visual cryptography suggests, it is related to the human visual system. When k pieces (shares) out of a total n are stacked together, the human eye performs the decryption. This gives rise to the k out of n visual cryptography scheme ((k,n)-VCS).

Visual cryptography is very secure and easily implemented. An electronic secret can be shared directly, alternatively the secrets can be printed out onto transparencies and superimposed, revealing the secret. The security of the scheme relies on a completely random one-time pad. If the pad is truly random and kept secret, perfect secrecy can be achieved [2][3]. This is another advantage of visual cryptography.

Naor and Shamir's initial implementation assumes that the image or message is a collection of black and white pixels; each pixel is handled individually. Newer schemes discussed later deal with grayscale and colour images which attempt to minimize the loss in contrast by using digital halftoning. Due to the fact that digital halftoning is a lossy process in itself [4], it is very hard to fully reconstruct the original secret image.

Below in Figure 1, the implementation and results of a $(2,2)$-VCS basic visual cryptography scheme are shown. It displays the secret image, the two generated shares and the recovery of the secret. Our proposed method of secret sharing

Y.Q. Shi (Ed.): Transactions on DHMS V, LNCS 6010, pp. 106–128, 2010.

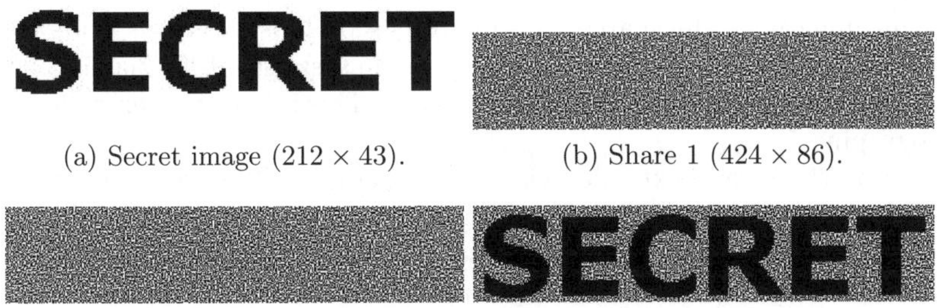

(a) Secret image (212 × 43).
(b) Share 1 (424 × 86).
(c) Share 2 (424 × 86).
(d) Restored image (424 × 86).

Fig. 1. The results of (2, 2)-VCS basic encryption process

expands on Naor's original findings in the 2-out-of-2 secret sharing scheme. The new method can be applied to a colour or grayscale image with an arbitrary number of layers (shares). Given a set of colours, this new method states that given any collection of $k - 1$ shares, no information on the colour of each pixel can be obtained, as well as the original images themselves.

In this paper, we will discuss how to generate two shares which can be used to hide multiple secrets. We refer to the second share in this paper as the "key" share. Using this key share, we can conceal multiple secrets within the first share, rather than a single secret, as per traditional visual cryptography. The "key" share stems from the idea of a master key. Traditionally, a master key is used to unlock many doors, each of which has their own unique corresponding key. We use this key share in the same way, in that it is used to recover different secrets from a single share.

Extending from this, we present a method for concealing different secrets in halftone and colour images. This idea initially stemmed from the masking technique used in Microsoft's Internet Explorer (IE). This mask occurs when the Select All option from the Edit menu is applied to any image currently opened within IE. The mask draws a blue mesh over the image. We attempt to combine and apply these ideas to the visual cryptography domain.

The remaining work is introduced as follows: we present the related work in Section 2; in Section 3 we introduce how to share multiple secrets; in Section 4 we discuss how to embed one of the generated shares into a halftone and colour image; Section 5 provides a security analysis of the proposed schemes; in Section 6 our experimental results are provided, including a sample web based VC system developed for these proposed schemes. The conclusion and future work are discussed within Section 7.

2 Related Work

Visual cryptography research has taken a great step since 1994. Originally, visual cryptography shared binary images; later on, researchers introduced halftone and colour halftone mechanisms to share colour [5] and grayscale [6] images.

Naor and Shamir [1] originally produced random patterns of dots with no visual meaning until the shares are superimposed. This raises suspicion of data encryption. Halftoning attempts to alleviate this suspicion by having visually pleasing attributes embedded within the shares. This is known as extended visual cryptography [7].

Based on the idea of extended visual cryptography, Zhou et al. [6] set about improving these techniques by proposing halftone grayscale images which carry significant visual information. This raises the suspicion of data encryption. To alleviate the suspicion of data encryption, halftone shares are created that carry one piece of information, such as another image, while having the secret hidden until all qualified shares are superimposed. This gives no indication that any encryption has been performed on each share. This in itself drastically improves the security model for visual cryptography. Along with Zhou, [8,9,10] present novel techniques by which halftone images can be shared with significant visual meaning which have a higher quality than those presented within [11] by employing error diffusion techniques [12]. These error diffusion techniques spread the pixels as homogeneously as possible to achieve the improvements in the shares overall quality.

A natural image halftone scheme [13] was proposed in which the quality of the shares are improved by using contrast enhancement techniques. However the problem with this scheme is that it is not perfectly secure. By using a space-filling curve ordered dithering technique [14], grayscale images can be converted into an approximate binary image. This allows encryption and decryption of the gray-level images using traditional visual cryptography methods [15].

Colour based VC schemes have also proven to be an important research area. An example finite lattice based structure consisting of all 8 colours from the CMYK-RGB colour model has been proposed [16]. After all the values (each separate colour) have been permuted in each of the 8 lattices, when the 2 shares are generated, the original image will be reproduced after the shares are superimposed. Since, in the above example there are $8 = 4 \times 2$ sub-pixels, the height or width of the image needs to be enlarged by a factor of two before the encryption. Each pixel in the original image is encrypted according to its colour. It is encrypted into an element randomly chosen from one of the lattices. Under such an encryption scheme, the two shares and the reproduced image become $16 = 4 \times 4$ times larger than the original image.

Novel schemes have also been proposed [17,18] which share colour images based on halftoning. With this halftone technology, different gray levels can be simulated simply by altering the density of the printed dots. Within bright parts of the image, the density is sparse, while in darker parts of the image, it is dense. This is helpful because a grayscale image can be transformed into a binary image. This allows for traditional visual cryptography techniques to be applied. Similarly, the colour decomposition method is used for colour images which also allows the proposed scheme to retain all the advantages of traditional visual cryptography, such as no computer participation required for the recovery of the secret.

Chang et al. [19] present a scheme based on smaller shadow images which permits colour image reconstruction when any authorized k shadow images are stacked together using their proposed revealing process. This improves on [20] which presents a scheme that reduces the shadow size by half. Chang et al.'s technique improves on the size of the share in that, as more shares are generated for sharing purposes, the overall size of those shares decreases.

The schemes previously discussed deal with sharing just one secret. So the natural extension of that is attempting to hide multiple secrets within a set of shares.

This problem was previously considered by Wu and Chen [21]. They concealed two secrets with two sets of shares S_1 and S_2. The first secret is revealed when S_1 and S_2 are superimposed. The second becomes available when S_1 is rotated anti-clockwise 90° and superimposed on S_2. Due to the nature of the angles required for revealing the secrets ($90°, 180°$ or $270°$) and the fact that this scheme can only share, at most, two secrets, it becomes apparent that it is quite limited in its use.

Multiple secret sharing was developed further [22] by designing circular shares so that the limitations of the angle ($\theta = 90°, 180°, 270°$) would no longer be an issue. The secrets can be revealed when S_1 is superimposed on S_2 and rotated clockwise by a certain angle θ, $0° < \theta < 360°$. A further extension of this was implemented in [23] which defines another scheme to hide two secret images in two shares with arbitrary rotating angles. This scheme rolls the share images into rings to allow easy rotation of the shares and thus does away with the angle limitation of Wu and Chang's scheme.

More recently, another novel multi-secret sharing scheme [24] was proposed that encodes a set of $x \geq 2$ secrets into two circle shares where x is the number of secrets to be shared. This is one of the first set of results presented that is capable of sharing more than two secrets using traditional visual cryptography. The algorithms presented can also be extended to work with grayscale images by using halftone techniques. Colour images could also be employed by using colour decomposition [5] or colour composition [25] techniques.

One difficulty with this scheme is the pixel expansion. The expansion that occurs is twice the number of secrets to be hidden, so the size of the circle shares increases dramatically when many large secrets are hidden. However, the number of secrets that are contained within the shares still remain a secret unless supplementary lines are added to the circle shares to ease the alignment. This is another problem with sharing multiple secrets, especially when dealing with circle shares, knowing the correct alignment points. Knowing how many secrets are actually contained within the shares is also a concern. Finally, the aspect ratio of the secrets becomes an issue. It isn't possible to share images using this technique without distorting the aspect ratio. We attempt to rectify this issue within this paper.

Our work presented within Section 3 differs from the current multiple secret sharing schemes in that we introduce a key share which is employed to share multiple secrets within a single share. Some of the new schemes presented keep the original aspect ratio of the secrets, meaning that the secrets can be reconstructed correctly, giving greater flexibility. Detailed within Section 4 is our proposed scheme which allows the use of halftone and colour images as a cover base to share visual cryptography secrets. We extend this by sharing multiple secrets within the base image and using the key share to decrypt them.

3 Sharing Multiple Secrets Using Visual Cryptography

Currently, the majority of research on visual cryptography is constrained on the scheme of single secret sharing. This new scheme outlines a novel approach to solving the problem of sharing multiple secrets using standard visual cryptography. This section focuses on how to share multiple secrets using visual cryptography.

Figure 2 illustrates the flowchart of our proposal. We merge two secrets into shares using a random pad, we combine s_1 from each secret to form a final share S_1, correspondingly, we modify s_2 from each secret and generate the new key share S_2. The new share S_1 and the key share S_2 are employed to recover the secrets by shifting the key share S_2 to various positions on S_1. S_2 will typically be referred to as the key share throughout the remainder of this paper.

It is also worth pointing out that a new key and random pad is generated for each new share. The same key is never used twice and every time the shares are encoded with this scheme, they will be completely different from the last time, even if the same image sets are used.

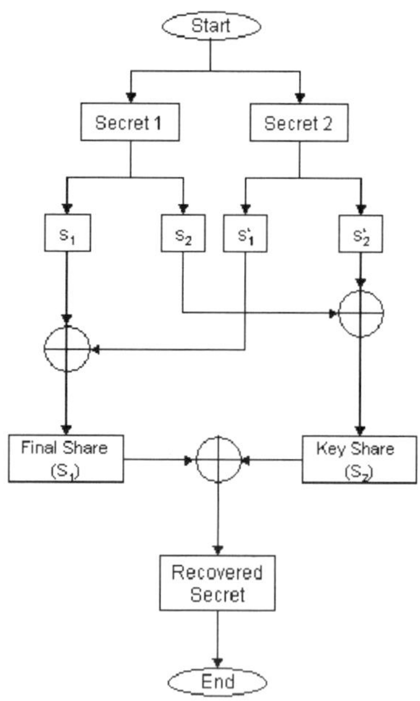

Fig. 2. Flowchart of the proposed multiple secret visual cryptography scheme

The multi-secret sharing scheme discussed within this paper is known generally as a joint sharing scheme, specifically, three different types of this scheme are proposed within this paper: **contrast based**, **even-odd based**, and **dynamic based**. Outlined below are the three different techniques used to accomplish this.

3.1 Contrast Based Joint Combination of Shares

Contrast based joint combination of shares is built on the idea that we can create multiple shares and one key share. By overlapping the shares to give one final share and by superimposing the key, the first secret is revealed. Shifting the key horizontally or vertically will reveal the other secrets.

Given the first secret, we write the pixels from the corresponding patterns of black pixels of the secret onto a blank image which is used as the combined share. For the second secret, we write the similar pixels on the blank region of the combined share. For the remaining regions on the combined share, we fill them up using the sharing patterns of white pixels. Mathematically, we can express this scheme by the following equations:

$$b^{w}_{b,w} = \begin{bmatrix} 1\,0\,1\,1 \\ 1\,1\,0\,1 \end{bmatrix} \tag{1}$$

$$b^{w}_{w,b} = \begin{bmatrix} 1\,0\,1\,1 \\ 1\,1\,0\,1 \end{bmatrix} \tag{2}$$

$$b^{w}_{w,w} = \begin{bmatrix} 1\,0\,1\,1 \\ 1\,0\,1\,1 \end{bmatrix} \tag{3}$$

where $b^{c}_{s_1,s_2} \in \{0,1\}$ is the pixel value of the share by the given pixel s_1 of secret 1 and s_2 of secret 2 with the pixel $c \in \{0,1\}$ of the cover image [7].

One solution to this problem can be implemented during the encryption process on each of the shares before they are overlapped. The process involves creating the first half of S_1 with a darker $\frac{3}{4}$ contrast to its upper half and creating the lower half of S_2 with a darker contrast when S_1 and S_2 are overlapped to generate the final share. This final share appears to be of a single contrast and does not give away any information about how many layers have been used in its creation. This scheme allows the secrets to keep their aspect ratio intact.

The disadvantage of this scheme is that it cannot share the secrets which have been made up fully of black pixels since the second secret will have no room for insertion into the rest space. The algorithm for generating these contrast based shares is detailed within Algorithm (1).

3.2 Even-Odd Joint Combination of Shares

Given two secrets with the same size, we can share them via two shares using a randomly generated pad. The two shares can be merged by filling the first share to the even rows of the combined image and the second share to the odd rows.

Algorithm 1. Joint contrast algorithm

Input: Two secrets I_1 and I_2
Output: Contrast visual cryptography shares S_1 and S_2
if $I_1.size = I_2.size$ **then**
  foreach *pixel* $(i, j) \in I_1$ **do**
    S_1 = pixelcodeTop(i, j);
    S_1 = randomly select pattern from $b^c_{s_1}$;
  end
  foreach *pixel* $(i, j) \in I_2$ **do**
    S_1 += pixelcodeBottom(i, j);
  end
  S_2 = generateKey();
  S_2 = randomly select pattern from $b^c_{s_2}$;
end
else
  Return an error. Images must be the same dimensions;
end
return S_1, S_2

The combined share will be twice the size of the secrets. Therefore, the final key share has to be adjusted in order to be capable of restoring the secrets.

Even-odd joint combination can generate any size of share. The difference between the even-odd joint combination and the contrast based combination of shares is that both shares are of the same size in the even-odd scheme. This helps to increase the capacity and security of the scheme as it gives away no indication as to the amount of secrets hidden related to the key size. The contrast of both shares in the even-odd scheme is also the same.

The encryption process works as shown in Figure 3. Two random keys are generated for encrypting both secrets. During this encryption, all the lines from secret one are written to the odd lines of the final share and secret two is written to the even lines with a two pixel gap. We need this gap because of the original sharing scheme that maps one pixel onto an array of 2×2. So row 0 and 1 will contain the pixels from secret one, row 2 and 3 will contain the pixels from secret two and so on, resulting in a final share that is twice as long. The resulting size depends on how many pixel spaces you want to write each time. In this example, one row is written per line, but it could be easily changed so that an arbitrary number of pixels are skipped. Correspondingly, we need to generate a key share which is combined from the even and odd lines of the set of second shares. When the combined key is superimposed on the final share and shifted up and down by two pixels, the secrets are revealed. The corresponding even-odd algorithm can be examined in Algorithm (2).

3.3 Dynamic Joint Combinations of Shares

This scheme takes into account the idea of hiding multiple images of a sequence within one share and moving the key share around the share to reveal the secrets.

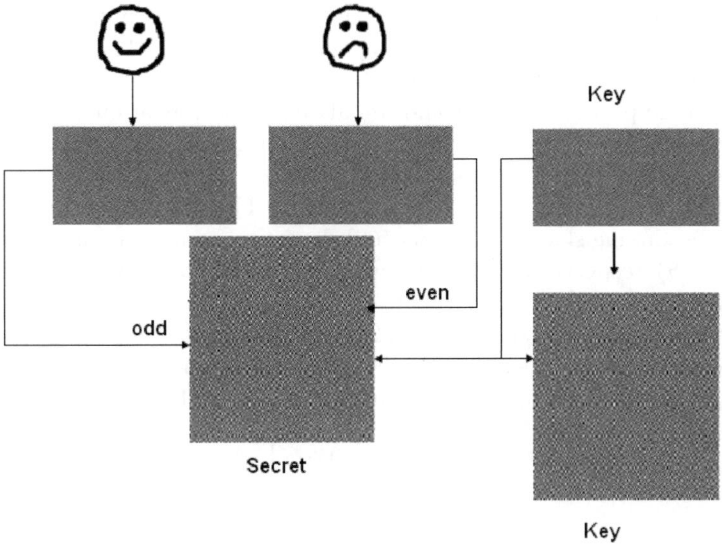

Fig. 3. The mechanism for even-odd joint combination of shares

Algorithm 2. Joint even/odd algorithm

Input: Two secrets I_1 and I_2 and the *pixelwidth* to skip
Output: Even/Odd visual cryptography shares S_1 and S_2

```
if I1.size = I2.size then
    foreach pixel (i,j) ∈ I1 do
        S1 = pixelcode(i,j);
        skip(pixelwidth);
    end
    foreach pixel (x,y) ∈ I2 do
        S1 += pixelcode(x,y);
        skip(pixelwidth);
    end
    S2 = generateKey();
end
else
    Return an error. Images must be the same dimensions;
end
return S1, S2
```

Dynamic joint combination of shares works as follows: one pixel from a secret is expanded into a 2×2 array. When these arrays are generated, they are moved to a larger image. We hide four secrets within the final share, it will be four times as large as the shares which get created per image.

In dynamic joint sharing, each pixel from secret one is converted to its 2×2 array and then placed into the group of four pixels in the final share. The same process is repeated for all other pixels in secret one. The same is done for the other three secrets, but they are offset by a certain amount. The same process is done when creating the key share, but the ordering is reversed. Without reversal simply superimposing the key would reveal all four secrets at once. As such, the key is shifted by four pixels (two pixels up or down, two pixels right or left) in each case to reveal the hidden secret.

So what we have happening is the following. The four secrets are split into their corresponding shares. Share one and share two from secret one are denoted as S_1^1 and S_2^1 respectively, therefore we generically represent the entire set of four shares as $S_{1,2}^i$ where $i = 1, \ldots, 4$.

These shares are then split into 2×2 pieces and placed into the final share in order to build it up. For example to illustrate this segmentation and placement into the final share, we can represent part of S_1^1 as per Eq. (4):

$$S_1^1 = \begin{bmatrix} 1 & 0 & \cdots \\ 0 & 1 & \cdots \\ \cdots & \cdots & \cdots \end{bmatrix} \tag{4}$$

This upper left section of share one, secret one $s_1^1 = \begin{bmatrix} 1 & 0 \\ 0 & 1 \end{bmatrix}$ of the share is then placed into a section of the final share F in order to reconstruct it. The same procedure is performed on the remaining 2×2 sections for the remainder of share one for secret one, through to share one for secret four. The final share begins to look something like Eq. (5):

$$F = \begin{bmatrix} s_1^1 & s_1^2 & \cdots \\ s_1^3 & s_1^4 & \cdots \\ \cdots & \cdots & \cdots \end{bmatrix} \tag{5}$$

The same procedure is used to build up the key share K, as per Eq. (6). However, the ordering is reversed. As previously mentioned, this is to stop all secrets being revealed at once.

$$K = \begin{bmatrix} s_2^1 & s_2^4 & \cdots \\ s_2^2 & s_2^3 & \cdots \\ \cdots & \cdots & \cdots \end{bmatrix} \tag{6}$$

The security of dynamic visual cryptography remains consistent with the original visual cryptography security. It is based on the protection of the shares no matter which dynamic scheme is employed. Obviously, dynamic visual cryptography makes the decryption much harder, the reason is that the merged share has multiple secrets hidden within and multiple alignment points have to be known before the secrets can be revealed.

3.4 Scheme Comparison

Each of the three schemes developed within this section has their own unique features. One of the main advantages of the contrast based sharing scheme along with the dynamic sharing scheme is that they keep the aspect ratio of the secret intact. The even-odd sharing scheme on the other hand alters the aspect ratio of the secrets. This is also the case with some of the previously discussed multiple secret sharing schemes that have been created.

Another important advantage of our contrast scheme and even-odd scheme are that the alignment points tend not to be such an issue. When the two shares are brought together and superimposed, the first secret can be successfully recovered. Depending on the orientation of the shares (vertical or horizontal), moving the top share in a vertical or horizontal direction will recover the remaining secrets. So, for example, in a vertical contrast based scheme (Figure 12), one superimposes the key share and then begins to move it down.

The dynamic scheme can be viewed in the same way, although the fact that there are four secrets and the fact that you have to move the key right, down, left and up again to recover each of the secrets is more complicated and not as practical.

This is a relatively simple solution to the alignment problem that these schemes are typically faced with. Although it can be time consuming to move the share slowly enough so that you do not miss any secrets, we believe it is an improvement over schemes which use supplementary lines on their shares.

This raises another point, determining how many secrets are actually hidden. If the number of secrets are to be kept a secret, then adding supplementary lines gives up the number of secrets. The number of secrets cannot be determined in our scheme as the shares appear to represent a single, traditional style of VC share. This area still warrants further investigation with regard to knowing the exact amount of secrets. The author's suggestion would be to have the number of secrets embedded into the final set of shares, so that when the first initial secret is recovered, there is also a number corresponding to the amount of secrets. Based on this number and the type of scheme, shifting the key in the corresponding direction will help recover the remaining secrets.

Finally, pixel expansion is discussed and compared against two other new schemes [22,24]. These schemes have a pixel expansion of four when it comes to sharing two secrets, that is, they end up with two shares, each of which consists of 256×256 pixels when two secrets of 128×128 are chosen. Our contrast scheme and even-odd scheme do not perform as well, each of which end up with 256×384 pixels and 256×512 pixels respectively when the same secret size is chosen.

However, in terms of sharing four secrets, [24] has an expansion of $2x$, where x is the number of secrets. Therefore sharing 4 secrets of 128×128 will require 512×512 pixels per share, which is equivalent to our dynamic scheme.

A main advantage of our scheme over the circular shares is that our scheme can share a wider range of secrets, images along with textual data. The aspect ratio is also kept intact with two of our schemes and no supplementary lines are required. Simply superimposing the shares will instantly recover the first secret. This could prove to be an issue when dealing with circular shares, due to the large number of angles of rotation.

4 Image Sharing Using Random Masks

Image hiding using colour images is a very interesting research topic since a lot of current information hiding techniques have various kinds of shortcomings. The robust schemes are very welcome in secret transmission implicitly. Using software for image editing or displaying, such as Microsoft Paint or Internet Explorer (IE) to robustly recover the secret is entertaining, albeit insecure.

Currently, one of the most robust ways to hide a secret within an image is by typically employing visual cryptography. The perfect scheme is extremely practical and can reveal secrets without computer participation. Recent state of the art watermarking [26] can hide a watermark in documents which require no specific key in order to retrieve it. We take the idea of unseen visible watermarks and apply a secure mask to them and incorporate it for use within the VC domain.

In this section, the transparent overlay (mask) mechanism in Internet Explorer is examined, in particular the Select All function within IE. Based on this, an interesting image hiding scheme is provided. The software will show viewers an interesting image which has been hidden in the original colour image (Figure 4(a)). If the Select All state is canceled, the original image will be restored. In other words, the original image and hidden image can be toggled using the Select All function of IE. The original image and the hidden image have the same resolution, but the content is completely different.

We take this mask mechanism and generalize it to allow hiding multiple VC shares within halftone and colour images which is completely independent of IE. The mechanism within IE is examined in Section 4.1; Sections 4.2 and 4.3 take this mechanism and apply it to different image types using visual cryptography. This allows us to use the VC shares as a secure mask for the halftone and colour

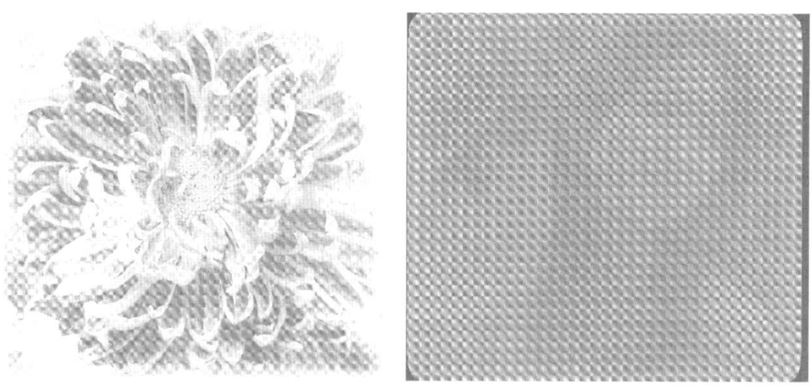

(a) An image downloaded from the internet.

(b) The image displayed by Microsoft's IE after the select operation.

Fig. 4. An example of image hiding using IE

images. This also allows for multiple secrets to be hidden within the base images. The results are presented within Section 6.3.

Figure 4 shows the Select All functionality. The flower image is opened using IE, the Select All function is chosen from the Edit menu and IE immediately shows a completely different image containing a woman. The ground truth of Figure 4 is that IE has a mask in its select operation. The mask is a fixed pattern which covers the currently visible part of the image and causes another image (of lower contrast) to appear. Utilizing this mask, it is possible to apply the same techniques to an animated GIF image if the Select All operation is triggered, the software has the potential to show another completely different animation. Using this detailed analysis, the mechanism of image hiding is introduced. This scheme is then propagated to a general situation and hides an animation in the colour images. The scheme is then extended further to general halftone and colour information hiding, which is capable of embedding the shares inside halftone and colour images. The techniques described are quite different from watermarking.

4.1 How to Hide an Image Using IE

From this observation, the transparent status of the Select All function in IE is quite interesting. In IE, the function has a fixed mask, and this mask is used to reach the transparent effect. The mask shown in Figure 5(a) can be discovered by opening a white image, and using the Select All function. If the mask is captured and zoomed, the ground truth can be found as to how the images are hidden. Figure 5(b) shows part of a completely red image that has been selected. From this mask, the IE select function is observed to use the mask like a chessboard directly covering on the image, only the white pixels in Figure 5(a) will be displayed, other pixels are blue. This is quite different from other browsers such as Mozilla's Firefox; it merges the blue channel with images shown in Figure 5(c).

After acquiring the basic principles of how the Select All function works these ideas are used to hide one image inside another and then using IE, the hidden image can be discovered. Given an image as the cover image, the pixel of the

(a) Open and select a white image using IE. (b) Open and select a red image using IE. (c) Open and select a red image using Firefox.

Fig. 5. An example of various browser masks

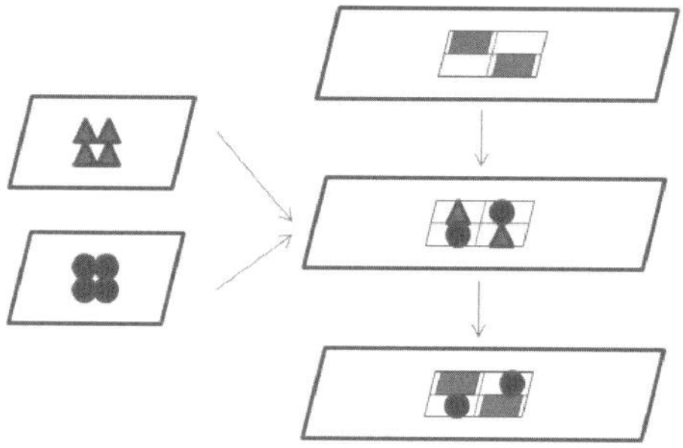

Fig. 6. Hiding colour images in another image and recovering the secret using the IE browser

public image at the blue pixel position of the mask in Figure 5(a) replaces the white pixels on the mask with the pixels on the secret image. If the corresponding pixels of the secret image are correctly positioned, the secret may be visible, therefore, the luminance of the image has to be adjusted and the contrast will be enhanced. Figure 6 shows how to merge two colour images together using the mask and transparent properties of the select function in IE. When the mask is covered on the merged image, the secret will be revealed and another completely different image is visible.

If the two colour images C^1 and C^2 have the same resolution, they can be represented as follows: $C^i = \{c^i_{j,k}\}$, $i = 1, 2$, $j = 1, 2, \cdots, W$ and $k = 1, 2, \cdots, H$, where W and H are the width and height of the image respectively and $c^i_{j,k}$ itself represents a pixel from C^i. The mechanism is as follows:

$$C^1 = \begin{bmatrix} c^1_{0,0} & c^1_{1,0} & \cdots & c^1_{W,0} \\ \cdots & \cdots & \cdots & \cdots \\ c^1_{0,H} & \cdots & \cdots & c^1_{W,H} \end{bmatrix} \tag{7}$$

$$C^2 = \begin{bmatrix} c^2_{0,0} & c^2_{1,0} & \cdots & c^2_{W,0} \\ \cdots & \cdots & \cdots & \cdots \\ c^2_{0,H} & \cdots & \cdots & c^2_{W,H} \end{bmatrix} \tag{8}$$

We then take C^2 and reduce its overall contrast by a factor of up to 70%. Then we merge the two images C^1 and C^2 together to represent the final merged image M which can be represented by:

$$M = \begin{bmatrix} c^1_{0,0} & c^2_{1,0} & \cdots & c^1_{W-1,0} & c^2_{W,0} \\ \cdots & \cdots & \cdots & \cdots & \cdots \\ c^2_{0,H} & c^1_{1,H} & \cdots & c^1_{W-1,H} & c^2_{W,H} \end{bmatrix} \tag{9}$$

Therefore, after the Select All operation, C^1 becomes masked and only the lower contrast C^2 is visible. This is why the image that is visible after the Select All operation has been performed must have a lower contrast and luminance. So it remains visually hidden until the higher contrast pixels of the other image are masked.

4.2 Embedding a Share of Visual Cryptography in a Halftone Image

Image hiding based on IE's select function provides the basis to hide the shares of visual cryptography in a halftone image. Figure 7 shows the two shares of an image "Q". Being able to hide these shares inside a halftone image without any noticeable changes in the base image would be highly desirable in terms of secret sharing.

(a) (b) (c)

Fig. 7. The "Q" image and its corresponding shares

Figure 8 shows the proposed halftone scheme and illustrates how to embed a share of visual cryptography into a halftone image. The halftone image is created using dispersed-dot ordered dithering [4]. Dispersed dots were chosen because they usually have a square shape, this corresponds to the square nature of the VC shares allowing a share to be inserted into a halftone image with minimal changes to the overall image.

With one of the shares in Figure 7, a similar region on the given image is searched for and the similar regions are employed to embed the share into this image using the even and odd scan lines. This merging combines the odd scan line from the share, the even scan lines from the public halftone image or visa versa. The merged image includes the secret, when another share of visual cryptography is overlapped on the regions, the secret is recovered.

Given the shares width W and height H, appropriate areas $W \times H$ are located within the base image. This involves working out the relative pixel densities with the shares D_{s_i}, s_1 and s_2 and the corresponding $W \times H$ area within the base image $D_{cW \times H}$. If the densities fall within a specific threshold ($T > 0$), then that is a potential area, suitable for hiding a share.

The difference at these locations is not noticeable because of the fact that only the odd lines from the share are written to the halftone image. This allows the halftone image to keep part of its pattern and shape, thus allowing the shares to blend in. That means the even lines from the halftone image fill in the missing lines from the embedded share. This has the potential to distort the recovered secret, however during our tests, this tends not to be the case. This is due to the threshold that is chosen. Because it leaves little room for error, any anomalous

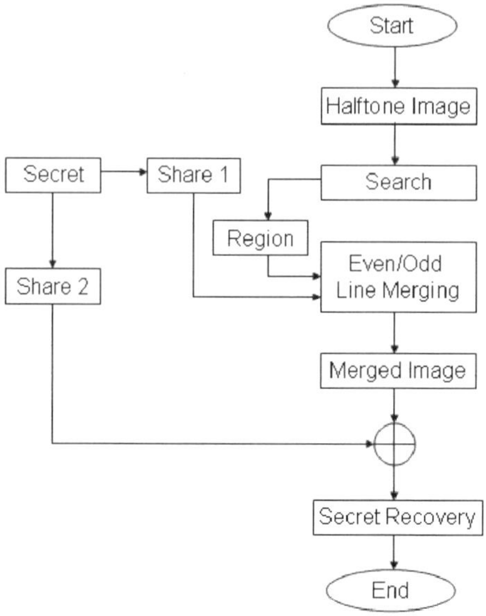

Fig. 8. Flowchart of secret hiding using visual cryptography

(a) (b)

Fig. 9. Comparison of pre (a) and post (b) share embedding

pixels recovered are not generally noticeable by the human visual system. When the comparison is done between the lines that get replaced in the halftone image by the lines in the shares, they appear quite similar. Figure 9 illustrates this minimal difference between the original and embedded image.

4.3 Embedding a Share of Visual Cryptography in a Colour Image

Correspondingly, the shares can be embedded into a colour image. It is possible to merge a binary share and a colour base image together. However, the merging mechanism is quite different from the halftone scheme. In this colour merging scheme, the shares are embedded completely within the colour image. The share is randomly based and it appears that the image could have some random noise on it. When the two shares are superimposed, the hidden secrets are restored. What is important is that the original colour image has minimal alterations.

The overall change is difficult to detect and in most cases the changes are not physically visible.

An objective way of testing the actual alteration between the original Lenna image and the Lenna image which contains the merged share is to use the peak signal-to-noise ratio (PSNR) metric to measure this difference.

The PSNR for an $n \times m$ colour image I and its noisy counterpart K is calculated thusly, first, the mean squared error (MSE) must be calculated on each pixel for each of its corresponding RGB channels using Eq. (10).

$$MSE = \frac{1}{nm} \sum_{i=0}^{n-1} \sum_{j=0}^{m-1} \|I(i,j) - K(i,j)\|^2 \tag{10}$$

After which, each channel's PSNR value must be calculated using Eq. (11). The values are then summed and averaged, resulting in the final PSNR value.

$$PSNR = 10 \cdot log_{10} \left(\frac{255^2}{MSE} \right) \tag{11}$$

The PSNR between the original image in Figure 16(a) and the image in Figure 16(c) is 21dB, which is an acceptable value of quality loss considering the images secure properties. Typically, for compressed colour images, the PSNR value lies between 30dB and 40dB.

The scheme works as follows, given a colour image and a binary share, the share is placed anywhere on the image. If the pixel on the colour image has a black pixel on top of it, that luminance of the colour image pixel $f(x, y)$ at location (x, y) is reduced. If the pixel on the superimposed share is white, skip it.

The security of embedding multiple secrets using visual cryptography in a halftone or colour image is higher than traditional visual cryptography. This is because halftone and colour images are introduced into visual cryptography as cover images and all the usual secure facts about visual cryptography remain unchanged.

The shares of traditional visual cryptography can arouse suspicion due to random noises, however, the halftone and colour images help to alleviate this suspicion due to their visual pleasing attributes.

5 Security Analysis

The proposed schemes developed within this section for hiding multiple secrets within a set of two shares are both secure and robust against many attack vectors.

The security of the proposed schemes can be attributed to the randomness of the shares. When representing black and white pixels, random permutations of those pixel representations are chosen. This allows the shares to be computationally secure against cryptographic analysis while separate. Consider the following:

Theorem 1. Our joint multiple secret sharing scheme is secure.

Proof. For arbitrarily chosen pixels on the original secret M, the pixels are either white (0) or black (1). We denote these as m_0 and m_1 respectively.

Considering the set of all possible pixel patterns for the shares, as each pixel is eventually encoded into one of the following patterns, this set is indeed the cryptogram space C.

Therefore we have the following:

$$M = \{0, 1\} \tag{12}$$

$$C = \{[1,1,0,0],[0,0,1,1],[1,0,0,1],[0,1,1,0],[1,0,1,0],[0,1,0,1]\} \tag{13}$$

Let c_j be the event that the share of four subpixels is the jth pattern of C, obviously $0 \leq j \leq 5$ and any c_j is equally probable. For a randomly picked secret image, we can assume that the pixel values are uniformly distributed, therefore $p(m_0) = p(m_1) = 0.5$. Consider either one of the shares. For any j, the pattern c_j can be merged with the same pattern c_j from the other share to construct a white (half-black) pixel; or it can be merged with its compliment $c_j + 1$ (if j is odd) or $c_j - 1$ (if j is even) to make up a fully black pixel. In other words, there is equal probability for the constructed pixel to be either white or black, so for any j, $p(m_0|c_j) = p(m_1|c_j) = 0.5$.

Hence for any i and j, we have $p(m_i|c_j) = p(m_i) = 0.5$, which completes our perfect cipher proof. This proof implies that visual cryptography schemes are indeed secure enough to be used in practice. □

Given two shares which contain multiple secrets, it is impossible for an attacker to know how many secrets are embedded. In a scheme involving two secrets and our even-odd scheme, even if an adversary was capable of extracting the salient pieces of information required which represents both secrets, superimposing them does not leak any information pertaining to the secrets. Figure 10 provides an example of this type of attack. Both secrets have been extracted into their own separate shares and then superimposed. No meaningful information is leaked whatsoever with this type of attack.

Binary images are very robust against attacks which are commonly used on images. Such attacks come in the form of image resizing, cropping, scaling, skewing and compression. After these attacks, the black pixels remain black and the white pixels remain white. Therefore binary images are a very good choice when it comes to protecting this type of data.

Scaling, cropping and image compression could also be attack vectors whereby an assailant attempts to get part of the secret to leak out. Figure 11 provides an example of a VC share which has been downsampled a number of times. It is obvious that no information pertaining to the secret is leaked. These images have also been compressed during their resize, this also confirms that the shares are not vulnerable to compression techniques.

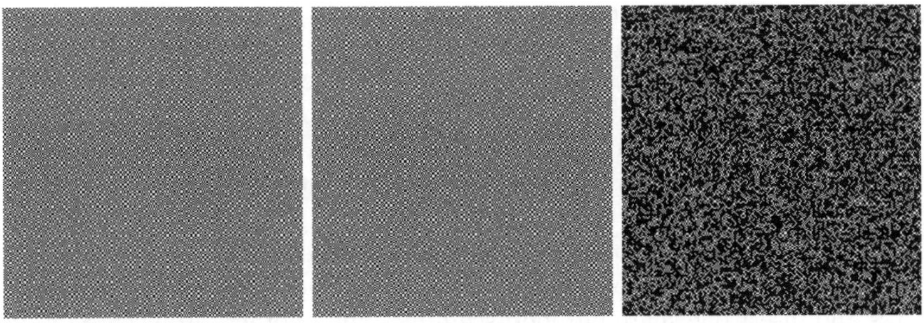

(a) Extracted share 1 (b) Extracted share 2 (c) Superimposing share 1 and share 2

Fig. 10. An attack vector on the Even-Odd scheme

(a) Original VC share 960×960. (b) Resized share 480×480. (c) Resized share 240×240. (d) Resized share 120×120. (e) Resized share 60×60.

Fig. 11. Results of resizing and compressing a VC share

6 Experimental Results

6.1 A Web Based VC System

Based on our work, a web based system was developed. Our experimental results can be downloaded from: http://www.cs.qub.ac.uk/~W.Yan/paper/DHMS.htm. The functionality of this software is introduced below:

- Basic VC: This provides the functionality of the original basic visual cryptography scheme.
- Joint VC: Another new scheme developed which allows images to be hidden using three different schemes; Contrast based, even/odd based and a sequence based approach. This is geared towards hiding multiple images within a single share.
- Colour VC: A new scheme that allows basic visual cryptography shares to be embedded inside a colour image. A sample decryption is also provided.

6.2 Joint Visual Cryptography Results

Given two secrets, the corresponding shares will be generated. The shares will be merged into one image, spatially. The challenge is to merge two shares that intersect. When the key share is superimposed on different positions of the merged share, the secret images will appear. One of our results with multiple secrets is shown in Figure 12. When the key is superimposed, secret 1 appears; when the key is shifted down to the bottom, secret 2 is revealed.

In order to merge multiple shares together, we extend the size of the merging shares and insert one share into odd scan lines and another into even scan lines shown in Figure 13. Correspondingly, the key share has to be extended. One of our results with multiple secret sharing is shown in Figure 14(a). Based on the four secrets (black bars), we generate a key share and a combined share

(a) Key share. (b) Combined contrast share. (c) Recovered secret one. (d) Recovered secret two.

Fig. 12. Joint contrast visual cryptography with two secrets

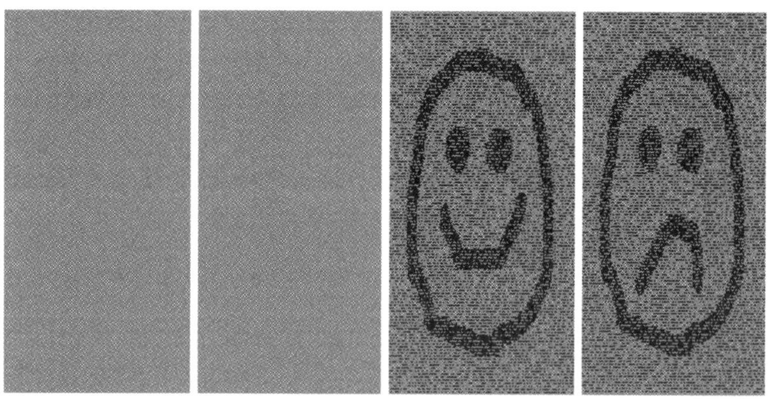

(a) Final share. (b) Key share. (c) Recovered secret one. (d) Recovered secret two.

Fig. 13. Joint visual cryptography based on even-odd combination of shares

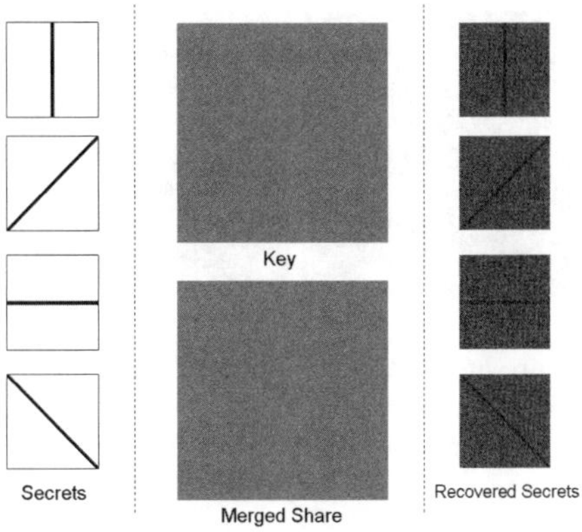

(a) Dynamic joint visual cryptography with multiple secrets (black bars).

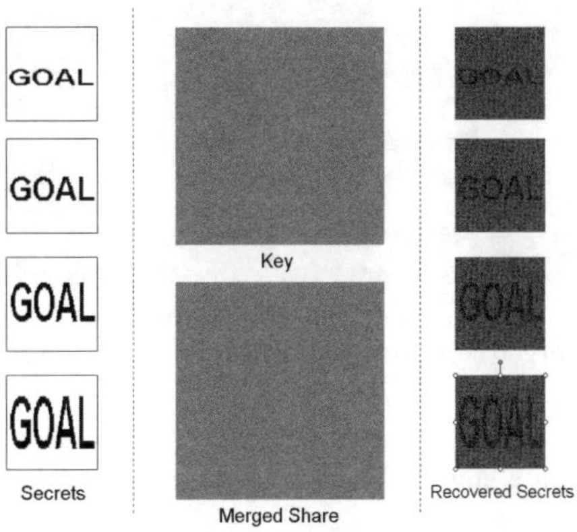

(b) Dynamic joint visual cryptography with multiple secrets (GOAL text).

Fig. 14. Results of a dynamic joint visual cryptography with multiple secret recovery

using the proposed scheme. When the key share is moved to different positions on the combined share, we can recover multiple secrets. The same is true for Figure 14(b) which also illustrates the secret recovery using the word "GOAL" which increases in size as the key share is moved around the merged share.

6.3 Random Mask Results

Given a halftone image and a number of shares, using the proposed halftone embedding scheme the shares are inserted into the image as best as possible. The most appropriate locations within the halftone images are selected. After the merging process is complete, the halftone image should be as unchanged as possible. After the embedding process is complete, the key share is used to recover one secret at a time. The results are detailed in Figure 15.

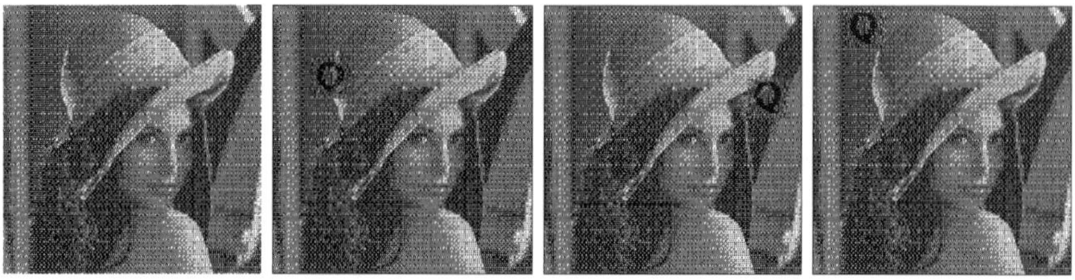

(a) Original image. (b) Embedded share at location 1. (c) Embedded share at location 2. (d) Embedded share at location 3.

Fig. 15. Embedding shares of visual cryptography into a halftone image

(a) Original colour image containing the merged share. (b) Visual cryptography key to superimpose. (c) Secrets revealed after superimposing (b) on the colour image.

Fig. 16. Merging a share of visual cryptography with a colour image

The colour example is detailed in Figure 16. In this example, the same share is embedded over the entire image, but having different shares using the same key is certainly possible. Superimposing the key share recovers the secrets. The various key shares are joined together, so all secrets are revealed at once.

7 Conclusion and Future Work

From the visual cryptography schemes proposed and demonstrated, it is possible to see that hiding secrets within images can prove to be highly advantageous. The best and most interesting results are gained when using a key that is the same size as the final share which may contain a number of different images. This makes it harder to determine whether the shares have actually been encrypted with just one hidden secret or with a large number of secrets.

The same is true when it comes to hiding visual cryptography shares inside halftone and colour images. This new scheme greatly improves the overall robustness of traditional visual cryptography because the halftone and colour images have very minimal changes after the adjustments have been made. Due to the fact that one of the schemes uses colour images, this gives it the potential for a wider range of applications.

Our future work will focus on multiple secret sharing using share rotation as well as using a revealing layer to locate the secrets. This is based on the ideas presented within [27] which use Band Moiré images to achieve these effects. Alternative print and scan tampering techniques will also be examined.

References

1. Naor, M., Shamir, A.: Visual Cryptography. In: De Santis, A. (ed.) EUROCRYPT 1994. LNCS, vol. 950, pp. 1–12. Springer, Heidelberg (1994)
2. Khan, D.: The Codebreakers: The Story of Secret Writing. Macmillan Publishing Co., New York (1967)
3. Schneier, B.: Applied Cryptography: Protocols, Algorithms, and Source Code in C. John Wiley & Sons, Inc., New York (1995)
4. Kang, H.R.: Digital Color Halftoning. In: Society of Photo-Optical Instrumentation Engineers (SPIE), Bellingham, WA, USA (1999)
5. Hou, Y.C.: Visual cryptography for color images. Pattern Recognition 36, 1619–1629 (2003)
6. Zhou, Z., Arce, G.R., Crescenzo, G.D.: Halftone visual cryptography. IEEE Transactions on Image Processing 15(8), 2441–2453 (2006)
7. Ateniese, G., Blundo, C., Santis, A.D., Stinson, D.R.: Extended Schemes for Visual Cryptography. Theoretical Computer Science 250, 1–16 (1996)
8. Myodo, E., Sakazawa, S., Takishima, Y.: Visual cryptography based on void-and-cluster halftoning technique. In: ICIP, pp. 97–100 (2006)
9. Myodo, E., Takagi, K., Miyaji, S., Takishima, Y.: Halftone visual cryptography embedding a natural grayscale image based on error diffusion technique. In: ICME, pp. 2114–2117 (2007)
10. Wang, Z., Arce, G.R.: Halftone visual cryptography through error diffusion. In: ICIP, pp. 109–112 (2006)
11. Ateniese, G., Blundo, C., Santis, A.D., Stinson, D.R.: Extended capabilities for visual cryptography. Theoretical Computer Science 250(1-2), 143–161 (2001)
12. Lau, D.L., Arce, G.R.: Modern Digital Halftoning. Marcel Dekker, New York (2000)
13. Nakajima, M., Yamaguchi, Y.: Extended visual cryptography for natural images. In: WSCG, pp. 303–310 (2002)
14. Zhang, Y.: Space-filling curve ordered dither. Computers & Graphics 22(4), 559–563 (1998)
15. Lin, C.C., Tsai, W.H.: Visual cryptography for gray-level images by dithering techniques. Pattern Recognition Letters 24(1-3), 349–358 (2003)
16. Koga, H., Yamamoto, H.: Proposal of a Lattice-Based Visual Secret Sharing Scheme for Color and Grey-Scale Images. IEICE Transation Fundamentals E81-A(6), 1262–1269 (1998)
17. Hou, Y.C., Chang, C.Y., Tu, S.F.: Visual cryptography for color images based on halftone technology. Image, Acoustic, Speech and Signal Processing, Part 2 (2001)
18. Prakash, N.K., Govindaraju, S.: Visual secret sharing schemes for color images using halftoning. In: Proceedings of the International Conference on Computational Intelligence and Multimedia Applications, ICCIMA 2007, Washington, DC, USA, pp. 174–178. IEEE Computer Society, Los Alamitos (2007)

19. Chang, C.C., Lin, C.C., Lin, C.H., Chen, Y.H.: A novel secret image sharing scheme in color images using small shadow images. Information Sciences 178(11), 2433–2447 (2008)
20. Yang, C.N., Chen, T.S.: New size-reduced visual secret sharing schemes with half reduction of shadow size. In: Gervasi, O., Gavrilova, M.L., Kumar, V., Laganá, A., Lee, H.P., Mun, Y., Taniar, D., Tan, C.J.K. (eds.) ICCSA 2005, Part I. LNCS, vol. 3480, pp. 19–28. Springer, Heidelberg (2005)
21. Wu, C., Chen, L.: A study on visual cryptography. Master's thesis, Institute of Computer and Information Science, National Chiao Tung University, Taiwan, R.O.C. (1998)
22. Wu, H.C., Chang, C.C.: Sharing visual multi-secrets using circle shares. Computer Standards & Interfaces 28, 123–135 (2005)
23. Hsu, H.C., Chen, T.S., Lin, Y.H.: The ringed shadow image technology of visual cryptography by applying diverse rotating angles to hide the secret sharing. Networking, Sensing and Control 2, 996–1001 (2004)
24. Shyu, S.J., Huang, S.Y., Lee, Y.K., Wang, R.Z., Chen, K.: Sharing multiple secrets in visual cryptography. Pattern Recognition 40(12), 3633–3651 (2007)
25. Shyu, S.J.: Efficient visual secret sharing scheme for color images. Pattern Recognition 39(5), 866–880 (2006)
26. Chuang, S.C., Huang, C.H., Wu, J.L.: Unseen visible watermarking. In: Proceedings of International Conference on Image Processing, San Antonio, USA, pp. 261–264 (2007)
27. Hersch, R.D., Chosson, S.: Band moiré images. In: ACM SIGGRAPH, pp. 239–247. ACM, New York (2004)

Author Index

Bouridane, Ahmed 1

Cha, Byung-Ho 34

Ito, Izumi 51

Kiya, Hitoshi 51
Kuo, C.-C. Jay 34
Kurugollu, Fatih 1

Laadjel, Moussadek 1

Metternich, Michael J. 18

Nibouche, Omar 1

Smeulders, Arnold W.M. 18

Weir, Jonathan 70, 106
Worring, Marcel 18

Yan, WeiQi 1, 70, 106

Printing: Mercedes-Druck, Berlin
Binding: Stein + Lehmann, Berlin